Wisdom's Many Faces

Wisdom's Many Faces

R. Charles Hill

A Michael Glazier Book
THE LITURGICAL PRESS
Collegeville, Minnesota

A Michael Glazier Book published by The Liturgical Press

Cover design by David Manahan, O.S.B.
Ravenna, mosaic, ca. 450. *Doves at a Fountain*, the so-called Mausoleum of
Galla Placidia.

1   2   3   4   5   6   7   8   9

Library of Congress Cataloging-in-Publication Data

Hill, Robert C. (Robert Charles), 1931–
    Wisdom's many faces / R. Charles Hill.
        p.   cm.
    "A Michael Glazier book."
    Includes bibliographical references and index.
    ISBN 0-8146-5515-7
    1. Wisdom literature.   2. Wisdom—Biblical teaching.   3. Wisdom—
Religious aspects—Christianity.   I. Title
BS1455.H55   1996
223'.06—dc20   95-40741
                                                                         CIP

Contents

Abbreviations

ABRL   Anchor Bible Reference Library

ANET   *Ancient Near Eastern Texts Relating to the Old Testament,* ed. J. B. Pritchard, 3rd ed. (Princeton: Princeton Univ. Press, 1969)

BZAW   *Beiheft zur Zeitschrift für die alttestamentliche Wissenschaft*

CBQ   *Catholic Biblical Quarterly*

CBQM   *Catholic Biblical Quarterly Monograph* Series

CCL   *Corpus Christianorum Latinorum*

HUCA   *Hebrew Union College Annual*

IDB   *The Interpreter's Dictionary of the Bible*

Int   *Interpretation*

JB   *Jerusalem Bible*

JBL   *Journal of Biblical Literature*

JBR   *Journal of Bible and Religion*

JSOT   *Journal for the Study of the Old Testament*

NAB   *New American Bible*

NJBC   *The New Jerome Biblical Commentary*

(N)RSV   *(New) Revised Standard Version*

OTL   Old Testament Library Series of Commentaries

OTRG   Old Testament Reading Guide Series of Commentaries

Q   *Quelle*

SJT   *Scottish Journal of Theology*

TWNT   *Theologisches Wörterbuch zum Neuen Testament,* ed. G. Kittel, English trans., *Theological Dictionary of the New Testament,* 10 vols. (Grand Rapids: Eerdmans, 1964-76)

VT   *Vetus Testamentum*

Preface

Perhaps it is unwise to accept the view of a discredited character like Zophar in the Book of Job that "wisdom is many-sided" (11:6). Yet that is the position adopted in this book, as its title suggests and the opening chapter explains. A warning is given not to latch onto one or another of Wisdom's many dimensions if we wish to do justice to this remarkable literature, biblical and extrabiblical, as a whole and to the distinctive worldview it incorporates.

Zophar's words may also serve as a disclaimer: the subject of Wisdom is more comprehensive than this book attempts to do justice to. A case is simply argued that we need to accept and hopefully even identify its many-sidedness if we are to appreciate Wisdom adequately. This could therefore not be described as one of many available introductions to Wisdom literature; rather, it presumes such a useful work has been digested and the reader is now in a position to follow a particular line of interpretation.

As often in advocacy exegesis, particular Wisdom texts and commentators have been selected for discussion of my thesis. The attempt has been made to present an intepretation clearly and simply while conducting most of the scholarly debate in endnotes. The general reader may choose as much or as little of the latter as suits.

Many of those who over the ages have claimed to be sage, whether by dint of experience or family position or merely age, have also fancied themselves as teachers. It could be proverbial that good learners make good teachers. Is the converse always true, that teachers learn much from their pupils? The Bible does not show that happening. And yet in the process of teaching it is not only the pupil who stands to learn from the interchange; I am indebted to many students over the years including most recently Gail Ball, Terry Grey, Mark McGrath, John Pentecost, and Andrew Watters for their sage comments. Sagacity and encouragement also from Raymond E. Brown, S.S., and Roland E. Murphy, O.Carm., have helped bring this book to publication.

1

Introduction:
The Quest for Wisdom

For all the accolades awarded it, the Book of Job in the Hebrew Bible presents a number of critical problems. While it has been variously classed as a literary masterpiece, one of the greatest works of world literature, the supreme achievement of Hebrew poetry, it also offers a text that is "the most vexed in the Old Testament"[1] and poses a basic question about the relationship of prose to verse sections and, in fact, to the book's overall literary integrity. The merit of Job, leaving aside both accolades and problems, is that it goes to the heart of biblical Wisdom.

The solution to Job's difficult lot lies not in the palpably facile moralizing of his friends or Elihu but in the nature of divine Wisdom—something more fundamental and comprehensive than mere human wisdom. So when in that "erratic intrusion,"[2] chapter 28 (an intrusion because jumping the gun of God's reply in chs. 38–41), Job twice puts the key question that is still inadequate: "where shall wisdom be found?" the book's true author replies at both those places in terms of a much deeper question: what is the nature of Wisdom?

It is an explanation that students of Wisdom often overlook because of being willing, like that book's characters, to settle for wisdom in their search for Wisdom. Hence the reason for this book.

1

In the New Testament generally, and in the Pauline corpus in particular, the notion and term "wisdom," *sophia,* occur frequently. This is principally because the composers like to see Jesus, or the whole mystery of Christ, succeeding to the characteristics of Old Testament wisdom, or Wisdom. One has only to read the opening chapters of 1 Corinthians to see the ambivalence (and the richness) that I am allowing for here and that Paul takes advantage of at that place.[3]

To clarify this point let us look at chapter 3 of Ephesians. The author, doing his best to establish his Pauline credentials, begins by speaking of his imprisonment; then in true Pauline fashion he goes off on a long digression about his missionary mandate based on his fresh insight into the mystery of Christ and his role in one dimension of this grand design, namely, bringing the Gentiles to share in it. The impression is effectively given that, as a Jew, he is profoundly moved by this shocking reinterpretation of a divine plan, a mystery, that he had been brought up to think much less comprehensive—in fact, confined to one racial group of beneficiaries. As he had done in chapter 1, he employs several synonyms for *mysterion,* "mystery," in this sense: "purpose," "plan," "will,"[4] and finally "wisdom," *sophia.* It is through the Church, he tells us, that this remarkable mystery will be made known and implemented.

A Polypoikilos *Wisdom*

It is not, he has come to realize, a simple "wisdom" any longer, a simple plan of salvation. There has, from a human and particularly Jewish point of view, been a fundamental reshaping of the divine intention. The beneficiaries are no longer simply Jewish; what had seemed a plain monochrome design now reveals its technicolor diversity and richness of texture. The author searches for a term to do justice to his startlingly expanded understanding. There is none at hand, so he coins one already rich in biblical associations. The term *poikilos,* which the Greek Bible had used of Joseph's fine but fateful coat in Genesis 37 and of the beautifully textured robe the Lord wove for his wanton daughter Jerusalem in Ezekiel's allegory (ch. 16) and which Peter then employed metaphorically of the Lord's wonderful range of gifts (1 Pet 4:10), is itself inadequate, so a neologism is required. The plan including Jew and Gentile has to be *multi*dimensioned, *multi*faceted, *multi*-colored, "of a rich variety":[5] a *polypoikilos sophia.*

It is a wonderful conviction and a profound theology by this New Testament theologian of the whole divine scheme of things, for which Wisdom—not simply wisdom—is an apt descriptor. Behind his adoption of that term (unique in the Bible) lies the multitude of concerns and characteristics and viewpoints of the sapiential composition of the Jewish Scriptures—a range of viewpoints that nevertheless together constitute a distinctive worldview readily distinguishable from that of prophets and historians and lawgivers and seers.[6] Sapiential composers are more than simply wise: theirs is truly a *poly-poikilos* outlook on the world and its inhabitants. Wisdom has many faces, if still a recognizable complexion.

R. E. Clements, who like many of us comes to Wisdom late in life, rightly speaks (as in our preface we saw Zophar doing: Job 11:6) of "the many-sidedness of Israelite wisdom,"[7] by which he means Wisdom, a typographical distinction one would wish (forlornly) to see maintained for the sake of clarity. How many sides, one might ask, how many faces does Wisdom offer us? They are numerous, and perhaps that is why in Proverbs 1–9 she sets up seven pillars or columns in building her house, as P. W. Skehan reminded us almost fifty years ago;[8] those carefully crafted chapters built on seven poems of uniform length reflect Wisdom's[9] diversity.

Wisdom's Seven Pillars

That is the contention of this book: that Wisdom—in the Bible and beyond it—has no exclusive concentration on wisdom but reveals a range of concerns and characteristics. Also, that these various concerns and aspects, which Ephesians calls *polypoikilos*, constitute a distinctive outlook or perspective, a recognizable sapiential worldview, and it is in this peculiar perspective that the essence of Wisdom lies—not in forms or anything equally superficial. The author of Job told us so long ago. The secret of life's problems is not to be found in human wisdom but in divine Wisdom—in the whole pattern of things, which does not surrender itself readily to human scrutiny, much though we like to play God and trot out pat solutions. Commentator Norman Habel well sums up Job's true message: "There are thus two sides to wisdom: the Wisdom hidden in the mysterious design of the cosmos and the wisdom which mortals seek so as to understand that design."[10]

In focusing on the peculiar perspective of sapiential composers in the Bible it is appropriate to keep in mind similar religious material by Jewish and Christian authors that did not finish up between those covers, such as the works variously styled but perhaps least problematically called "intertestamental," also gnostic scriptures and works by the Qumran community. In addition, if only because of undoubted influence on biblical composers,[11] extrabiblical literature from Egypt, in Akkadian and Sumerian from Mesopotamia, in Canaanite and Phoenician, helps fill out the picture of Wisdom in the Near East in the biblical period.

It is as interesting and relevant to note (as we shall) the degree of correspondence of viewpoints between biblical and extrabiblical sages as it is to ask the question Where do we look for today's Wisdom? Who are today's sages? Do we find a perspective similar to Proverbs and Sirach in the modern bestseller *Life's Little Instruction Book: 477 Suggestions, Observations, and Reminders on How to Live a Happy and Rewarding Life*[12] or in the monthly issues of the *Reader's Digest?* Or is it to talk radio that people turn for a contemporary sage?

In Quest of Wisdom

We are definitely off on the wrong foot in quest of the true nature of Wisdom if we proceed nominally, as does R. N. Whybray, with a word search. "We may begin by attempting to discover what the Israelites themselves called 'wisdom,' and whom they regarded as 'wise,'" he tells us[13] and proceeds to follow his own advice. That may work for a mere substantive like "covenant" or "truth" but not if we are trying to sum up the distinctive character of a whole body of literature of varying provenance and the tradition on which it rests; we have to be more discerning and less mechanical. Predictably, Whybray concludes from his word search that one of the main characteristics of Wisdom is "its intellectual or ratiocinative quality."[14] Gerhard Von Rad in his second attempt to pin Wisdom down[15] still falls far short of the mark in speaking of it as "Israel's didactic literature," "the didactic books of the Old Testament,"[16] and perhaps aware that these terms do not suffice, adds that "the concept 'wisdom' has become increasingly unclear" and wonders "whether the attractive code-name 'wisdom' is nowadays not more of a hindrance than a help."[17] Even as experienced a commentator as James Crenshaw can settle for "hagiographic,"[18] alongside Whybray's "intellectual" and Von Rad's "didactic." So much for the adequacy of nominal definitions and one-liners in an endeavor that is *polypoikilos*.[19]

If we fall into that trap, we are not listening to the Book of Job on the correct understanding of Wisdom. Nor are we if we settle for only one face of Wisdom's many faces, one superficial characteristic of the body of sapiential material, such as forms like the *mashal*. Roland E. Murphy, who has spent a lifetime on biblical Wisdom, has consistently reminded us that his subject is "both content and style" (as he says in a recent treatment),[20] just as he began a similar introduction a quarter of a century before with (Old Testament) Wisdom's "literary characteristics," particularly the proverb.[21] Though he is impatient of Whybray's nominal approach, it could also be said to him, as to those who look to proverb and parable for traces of Wisdom in Jesus' mouth,[22] that forms are but an element of the picture.

Not only that, but the formal aspect of Wisdom has become so diffuse, as scholars suggest the influence of sages in an ever-expanding range of literary types—not just proverb and riddle, parable and fable, but numerical formulae and allegory, dialogue and autobiographical narrative, hymns and laws, didactic narrative and prohibitions, psalms and woe oracles, even torah and apocalyptic. Are we brought to acceptance of Von Rad's conclusion that reference to "Wisdom" at all has become "more of a hindrance than a help" and, with James Crenshaw, that "the cumulative effect of such endeavors renders wisdom diffuse beyond recognition"?[23]

Many Faces, One Perspective

No: the formal aspect of Wisdom is but one of its faces and far from its most characteristic; we shall look at this in chapter 11. Rather, we ought to heed the advice of those who direct our attention to its many faces and to a more integral quest, like Crenshaw himself, who believes at least of Old Testament Wisdom that it "constitutes [is constituted by?] a body of literature, a way of thinking, and a tradition";[24] elsewhere he surveys a range of definitions.[25] We recall Murphy's accent on Wisdom's "typical approach to reality."[26] Von Rad suggests a "way of thinking,"[27] and E. H. Heaton holds for "neither a similar theological purpose nor a fixed literary genre but rather an identifiable intellectual stance and literary idiom."[28] Donn Morgan, who is interested in Wisdom influences in other bodies of Old Testament material, notes the wider view now being taken of Wisdom, "a movement, a way of life, a way of thought and speech."[29]

At least in these attempts to measure up to all that Wisdom offers there is some recognition that a range of characteristics and aspects is involved in sapiential material, perhaps least of all the formal. There is a general acceptance that a particular worldview is characteristic of the sages; the world is seen in somewhat different terms from its perception by prophets or apocalyptic visionaries or lawmakers or historians, whatever forms these composers chose to convey their perceptions and concerns. In other words, there is a typical Wisdom perspective on people and the world, a complex and manifold perspective for which *polypoikilos* is a fair description with its suggestion of all the many dimensions of Wisdom. Those many facets and dimensions need distinguishing in order for us to grasp the sapiential perspective fully; the following chapters proceed in that way. First, however, there are some further general remarks to be made about the quest for Wisdom.

Neglect of Biblical Wisdom

Acknowledgment should be made that today there is a growing degree of attention to biblical Wisdom in scriptural scholarship and that, concomitantly, scholars are looking to sapiential accents in extrabiblical literature. In fact, as is suggested above by the excesses in unearthing Wisdom accents and forms throughout the Bible where they might not reasonably have been expected, perhaps we have reached an unhealthy pan-sapientialism. The pendulum has swung too far from an earlier time when it was thought irrelevant to true biblical scholarship to take account of the works of the sages as distinct from Torah and Prophets. I recall directing my attention to Wisdom in the 1960s and having to cope with discouragement from the great tradition historians like Von Rad and his disciples for its failure to conform to the concerns and patterns of those other composers.[30]

For Von Rad Wisdom, in comparison with pentateuchal cultic credos, was "slightly tinged with the pallor of theological reflexion."[31] Consequently, his disciples settled, like him, for a canon within the canon; Wisdom was excluded (in the words of G. Ernest Wright) "because it does not fit into the type of faith exhibited in the historical and prophetic literatures,"[32] which had become the norm for all biblical statement. Wright could, on this same rationale and by an inverted logic, go so far as to ignore Wisdom's conspicuous contributions to biblical thought and claim that "the difficulty of the wisdom movement was that its theological base and interest were too narrowly fixed"![33] Such scholars, whether from conviction or under the influence of the scholarly giants of the day, decided on an (inadequate) biblical worldview and eliminated Wisdom from sharing it. John Bright in 1967 concurred: "Some parts of the Old Testament are far less clearly expressive of Israel's distinctive understanding of reality than others, some parts (and one thinks of such a book as Proverbs) seem to be only peripherally related to it, while others (for example Ecclesiastes) even question some of its essential features."[34] One's skepticism of scholarly fads is reinforced!

Even those in this period, like Roland Murphy, who persisted in their disreputable interest in Wisdom, could speak as he did in 1965 of "the omissions in the wisdom literature,"[35] which again implies a norm or canon from which Wisdom disqualifies itself. A recent convert, R. E. Clements, who has lately published more than once on Wisdom, admits that as late as 1980 he produced a volume on Old Testament theology that took no account of the importance of the Israelite Wisdom tradition.[36] Other latter-day scholars have surveyed this period of neglect and prejudice, speaking of Wisdom as the Cinderella of biblical studies[37] or as the orphan who has now become a queen (if only queen for a day, one warns).[38] There were those in the earlier period who protested at this unjustified suppression of valid biblical viewpoints, like L. E. Toombs[39] in 1955 and J. F. Priest[40] in 1962; and eventually the tide turned and has become a veritable tidal wave, though as late as 1992 a book could still be written entitled *The Old Testament of the Old Testament*[41]—a title sounding suspiciously like "the canon within the canon"—that ignores Wisdom books completely.

The prospects of the tidal wave receding, or the queen being dethroned, or pan-sapientialism gaining some balance, are not bright, it would appear. The concerns of Wisdom, particularly anthropological and cosmic, relate closely to those of our contemporaries. Christology and cosmology have accordingly found biblical and extrabiblical Wisdom grist to their mill.[42] The Sophia movement is gaining strength as well; Wisdom speaks appealingly to feminist aspirations. A book has just come to my desk for review entitled *Wisdom and Demons*[43] in which sapiential ideas are related to exorcism; the mind boggles at further possibilities. One would hope that in this fervor of replacing previous neglect the true perspective of Wisdom and its many faces are discerned.

The Extent of Wisdom

Happily, one issue that contributed to the marginalizing of biblical Wisdom books in earlier decades—their deutero-canonical status—has ceased to matter. This is especially due to a rethinking of the factors that led to the determination of biblical canon in the first place, thanks to the work of Protestant scholars like Albert C. Sundberg[44] and James A. Sanders.[45] In 1936 O. S. Rankin in *Israel's Wisdom Literature* lamented its neglect, which he put down partly to canonical status and partly to the fact that it seemed "mundane and pedestrian."[46] He himself shook off both these obstacles and wrote perceptively of the several characteristics that compose the distinctive Wisdom perspective.[47]

Today a prolific writer on Wisdom, James Crenshaw, feels the need (in choosing for his study Proverbs, Job, Qoheleth, Sirach, Wisdom of Solomon, and some Psalms) to defend not their canonical status but the exclusion of other texts like the Joseph narrative or the Succession narrative, admitted as sapiential by other scholars.[48] He is therefore at a great advantage in arriving at an appreciation of Wisdom's many faces in comparison with someone like Walther Zimmerli, who in 1964 chose to confine his still-influential study[49] to Proverbs and Ecclesiastes and who, as we shall see, came to some unfortunate conclusions. One likewise regrets the limited scope of

Gerald T. Sheppard, who as recently as 1980 concentrated on Sirach and Baruch to study Wisdom as a hermeneutical construct, or theological concept, for interpreting sacred Scripture.[50] Omission of Paul or James in considering New Testament Wisdom would be equally myopic.

The intention in this present work, on the contrary, is to consider all the biblical Wisdom material and to contextualize it by also looking at other bodies of religious composition in the biblical period and somewhat before it. To avoid the danger of circular reasoning in this, to which Crenshaw alerts us,[51] we shall make biblical Wisdom our paradigm; yet, in light of the wider corpus of material, that decision—what is Wisdom and what are its many faces—should be arrived at in a more enlightened fashion.

Sages and Settings

To some, however, this procedure would not be sufficiently discriminating: even within the Bible there is "wisdom" and "Wisdom." Old Testament Wisdom can be "old," "late," apocalyptic; depending on the period and its exponents and practitioners, it can take the form of the pragmatic art of statesmanship, or ethics and theology, or esoteric knowledge and secret lore.[52] Hence scholars look closely at the sages and the institutions and life situations where they exercised their craft, if craft it was. Was it a courtly occupation? Certainly Solomon becomes the paradigmatic sage, and it is instructive to see both the encomium of him in 1 Kings and the New Testament's claim that in Jesus something similar, if greater, has come:

> God gave Solomon very great wisdom, discernment, and breadth of understanding as vast as the sand on the seashore. . . . He composed three thousand proverbs, and his songs numbered a thousand and five. He would speak of trees, from the cedar that is in the Lebanon to the hyssop that grows in the wall; he would speak of animals, and birds, and reptiles, and fish. People came from all the nations to hear the wisdom of Solomon (4:29, 32-34).

Jesus as sage would couch his teaching in similarly sapiential terms—birds of the air and foxes, good trees and bad fruit, flowers of the field and old wine; this rather than proverb or parable or courtly setting distinguishes his style.

Or do the roots of biblical Wisdom lie in the family? or the clan? or in schools, whether scribal schools or Temple schools or court schools? Were the sages scribes or intellectuals?

Much biblical Wisdom is something that can be communicated and learned as the fruit of experience. Fathers often so speak to sons, as do mothers (to daughters?):

> Hear, my child, your father's instruction,
>> and do not reject your mother's teaching (Prov 1:8; cf. 4:3;
>> 6:20; Sir 8:9).

Proverbial material in popular Wisdom also makes reference to kings and courtly behavior, even in postexilic Wisdom after Israel's monarchy had ceased to exist—perhaps out of a sense that due order must be preserved no matter which power was in possession.[53] The prophets at various times seem to recognize in the sages a class of people, not only in Israel but also in Egypt and Edom, and often find them arrogant and misleading; so, for example, Isaiah of Jerusalem, Jeremiah, Ezekiel, Obadiah:

> How can you say, "We are wise,
>> and the law of the Lord is with us,"
> when, in fact, the false pen of the scribes
>> has made it into a lie?
> The wise shall be put to shame,
>> they shall be dismayed and taken;
> since they have rejected the word of the Lord,
>> what wisdom is in them? (Jer 8:8-9; cf. 18:18).[54]

Did the sages at any stage conduct schools in Israel? Only at the very end of Sirach in the second century is there any textual support for the idea:

> Draw near to me, you who are uneducated,
>> and lodge in the house of instruction (51:23).

Scribal educators are known to have operated in Temple schools in Egypt, Babylonia, Sumer, and Ugarit, and for that reason an assumption is sometimes made that biblical Wisdom grows out of that setting too.[55] But Israel's Wisdom develops at a later period, making the assumption doubtful.[56] We are on safer ground in recognizing some development in what was originally folk Wisdom without achieving clarity as to its setting outside family and clan prior to Sirach. That development, theological and religious and traditional, we can note as we study each of Wisdom's many faces.

Notes

1. M. Pope, "Job," *Anchor Bible,* 3rd ed. (Garden City: Doubleday, 1973) 15:xliii.

2. Cf. N. Habel, *The Book of Job,* OTL (Philadelphia: Westminster, 1985) 391. See also my "Job in Search of Wisdom," *Scripture Bulletin* 23, no. 2 (1993) 34–38.

3. Some of the distinctions involved here and their Christological significance I have tried to develop in *Jesus and the Mystery of Christ* (Melbourne: CollinsDove, 1993).

4. The writer speaks also of *oikonomia,* the plan in operation (3:9). Such terms are discussed in my "Mystery of Christ: Clue to Paul's Thinking on Wisdom," *The Heythrop Journal* 25 (1984) 475–83.

5. So the *NRSV,* nicely, expressing diversity of both color and texture (the *RSV*'s "manifold" was insipid).

6. Admittedly, parts of the Wisdom of Solomon strike one as more apocalyptic than sapiential: cf. 4:16ff.; 5:15-23.

7. *Wisdom for a Changing World: Wisdom in Old Testament Theology* (Berkeley: BIBAL, 1990) 15.

8. "The seven columns of Wisdom's house in Proverbs 1–9" (a paper first composed in 1946, Skehan admits) in *Studies in Israelite Poetry and Wisdom,* CBQM 1 (Washington: Catholic Biblical Association of America, 1971) 9–15. Skehan tells us: "Columns, we should say, and not pillars, in order to secure in English the meaning of the author" (9).

9. Wisdom in upper case in this and similar references to Lady Wisdom, where wisdom is personified or hypostatized (an issue to be addressed in ch. 3), is a different referent from Wisdom as a body of lit-

erature or peculiar worldview in the sense we have explained.

10. The Book of Job, 544. Job, of course, is not our only biblical paradigm. Qoheleth, too, "king over Israel in Jerusalem" and therefore an obligatory champion of wisdom (Eccl 1:12), is nevertheless convinced of its severe limitations (1:12-18; 2:21; 6:8); but—grudgingly and dyspeptically—he concedes a pervasive universal Wisdom in things (5:18; 6:6; 7:14; 8:16-17; 11:5; 12:14).

11. We are much less confident today than a Von Rad or an Albright of a close relationship of biblical works, like Proverbs, to earlier, similar material from those influential neighbors. We would not be so ready to admit with the former "the discovery that a whole passage from the wisdom book of Amenemope had been taken over almost word for word into the biblical book of Proverbs (Prov 22:17–23:11)" (*Wisdom in Israel*, 9) or, with Albright, posit strong verbatim Canaanite and Phoenician influence on Proverbs, Job, Ecclesiastes ("Some Canaanite-Phoenician Sources of Hebrew Wisdom" in M. Noth, D. W. Thomas, eds., *Wisdom in Israel and in the Ancient Near East* [*VT* Supp. 3, Leiden: Brill, 1960] 1–15).

This is not to discount the value of studying what M. Dahood calls "the Canaanite connection" or to stand Canute-wise against "une vague 'eblaïtique'" (see his article "Eblaite and Biblical Hebrew," *CBQ* 44 [1982] 1–24).

12. H. Jackson Brown, Jr. (Melbourne: Bookman, 1991).

13. *The Intellectual Tradition in the Old Testament* (Berlin and New York: De Gruyter, 1974) 5.

14. Ibid., 2.

15. In *Wisdom in Israel* (1970), English trans. (London: SCM, 1972), after his unsympathetic presentation of it in his *Old Testament Theology*, vol. 1 (1957), English trans. (Edinburgh and London: Oliver & Boyd, 1963).

16. *Wisdom in Israel*, x, 7. William Albright speaks in similar terms (art. cit.).

17. Wisdom in Israel, 7, 8.

18. "Method in determining Wisdom influence upon 'historical' literature," *Studies in Ancient Israelite Wisdom*, J. L. Crenshaw, ed. (New York: Ktav, 1976) 481.

19. One might add as a corollary that while the Wisdom of Solomon flaunts its sapiential character in its title, it is probably the least sapiential of the commonly nominated Wisdom books.

20. *NJBC* (1990) 447. In his *Tree of Life: An Exploration of Biblical Wisdom Literature,* ABRL (New York: Doubleday, 1990), in discouraging Whybray's nominal approach, Murphy sees Wisdom rather consisting of "the typical approach to reality and the specific literary forms that can be found" in Wisdom material (1). He can also warn against use of the term "wisdom literature" as misleading in directing attention solely to literary remains, ironically in a book called *Wisdom Literature (The Forms of Old Testament Literature* 13) (Grand Rapids: Eerdmans, 1983) 3.

21. *Introduction to the Wisdom Literature of the Old Testament,* OTRG 22 (Collegeville: The Liturgical Press, 1965) ch. 1.

22. Cf. W. A. Beardslee, "Uses of the Proverb in the Synoptic Gospels," *Interpretation* 24 (1970) 61–73.

23. "Wisdom in the OT," *IDB,* 953.

24. Ibid., 952.

25. "Prolegomenon," *Studies in Ancient Israelite Wisdom,* 3–5.

26. In his "Wisdom—Theses and Hypotheses," *Israelite Wisdom,* ed. J. G. Gammie and others (Missoula: Scholars Press, 1978) 39, he speaks also of "an approach to reality."

27. *Wisdom in Israel,* 291.

28. *Solomon's New Men* (New York: Pica, 1974) 130.

29. *Wisdom in the Old Testament Traditions* (Oxford: Blackwell, 1981) 22.

30. See my "Dimensions of Salvation History in the Wisdom Books," *Scripture* 19 (1967) 97–106.

31. *Old Testament Theology* 1:446.

32. *God Who Acts: Biblical Theology as Recital,* Studies in Biblical Theology 8 (London: SCM, 1952) 103.

33. Ibid., 104.

34. *The Authority of the Old Testament* (London: SCM, 1967) 136.

35. *Introduction to the Wisdom Literature of the Old Testament,* 35–36. Murphy concedes: "It still remains true that, relatively speaking, the sages ignore what is peculiarly Israelite" (36). It was some years later that Murphy was noting among scholars the opposite attitude: "Now the question would rather be, where has Old Testament wisdom failed to appear?" ("The Interpretation of Old Testament Wisdom Literature," *Int* 23 [1969] 290).

36. *Wisdom in Theology* (a revision of his 1990 *Wisdom for a Changing World;* see n. 7 above) (Grand Rapids: Eerdmans, 1992) 7.

37. R. Davidson, *Wisdom and Worship* (London: SCM, 1990) 11.

38. Crenshaw, "Prolegomenon," 3.

39. "Old Testament and the Wisdom Literature," *JBR* 23 (1955) 193–96.

40. "Where Is Wisdom to Be Placed?" *Studies in Ancient Israelite Wisdom,* 281–88.

41. R.W.L. Moberly (Minneapolis: Fortress, 1992). The only textual references to Wisdom books (Prov, Job, Eccl) occur on page 101 in a reference to R. Otto's *The Idea of the Holy*. For Moberly the Yahwist is the core of the OT.

42. See my *Jesus and the Mystery of Christ*. Not all contemporary studies of this kind show an adequate understanding of Wisdom's many faces as distinct, say, from an interest in Lady Wisdom: cf. M. Fox, *The Coming of the Cosmic Christ* (Melbourne: CollinsDove, 1989).

43. By D. A. Lee and J. Honner (Melbourne: Aurora, 1993).

44. *The Old Testament of the Early Church* (Cambridge, Mass.: Harvard Univ. Press, 1964); "Reexamining the Formation of the Old Testament Canon," *Interpretation* 42 (1988) 78–82.

45. *Canon and Community: A Guide to Canonical Criticism* (Philadelphia: Fortress, 1984).

46. *Israel's Wisdom Literature* (1936) (New York: Shocken, 1969) vii.

47. "Though interest in morality and religion is common to prophetic, apocalyptic, and other forms of composition, there is in the Wisdom writings a quite distinctive quality of mind, method, and outlook in respect of ethics and religious belief" (ix).

48. "Prolegomenon," 5. For Crenshaw Wisdom has thrown off "the stigma of deutero-canonicity" (3); in fact, one could say the stigma has become their stigmata! He is equally catholic in his *Old Testament Wisdom: An Introduction* (Atlanta: John Knox, 1981).

49. "The Place and Limit of Wisdom in the Framework of Old Testament Theology," *Scottish Journal of Theology* 17 (1964), reprinted in Crenshaw, *Studies in Ancient Israelite Wisdom,* 314–26.

50. *Wisdom as a Hermeneutical Construct: A Study of the Sapientializing of the Old Testament,* *BZAW* 151 (Berlin and New York: Walter de Gruyter, 1980).

51. "Wisdom in the OT," *IDB,* 953: "We begin with an entity that we choose to label 'wisdom,' and work from it. We then exclude texts that differ essentially from that normative corpus of literature. Everything hinges upon the accuracy of our initial decision. Precisely at this point, comparison with non-Israelite wisdom literature becomes

both an asset and a liability." There will be no exclusion here, at least of biblical material (such as we regretted in the tradition historians' approach to the canon).

52. So say scholars like W. McKane, *Prophets and Wise Men*, rev. ed. (London: SCM, 1983), and Von Rad, *Wisdom in Israel*—though McKane would not share all Von Rad's positions (cf. *Prophets and Wise Men*, 48–53).

53. So Clements, *Wisdom for a Changing World*, 72.

54. McKane would see this as prophetic rejection of "old wisdom," pragmatic, unethical, irreligious (*Prophets and Wise Men*, 47, 65ff.). Morgan sees it rather differently: "The basic disagreement seems to center on the ultimate basis of one's loyalty, whether state or nation or Yahweh" (*Wisdom in the Old Testament Traditions*, 90).

55. So McKane, *Prophets and Wise Men*, 36, and Von Rad, *Wisdom in Israel*, 17. Michael V. Fox, "The Pedagogy of Proverbs 2" (*JBL* 113, no. 2 [1994] 233) speaks freely of "schools" in connection with the world of Proverbs.

56. "The emergence of Israel on the historical scene came centuries later than the heyday of schools in either Egypt or Mesopotamia" (Crenshaw, "Education in Ancient Israel," *JBL* 104 [1985] 609). Morgan, too, who surveys the evidence thoroughly (in *Wisdom in the Old Testament Traditions*), urges caution.

2

The Human Face of Wisdom

Unlike the historical incarnation, the Word of God who reaches us in the text of the Bible does not always present a human face. Even less appealing is the limited biblical canon that scholars have concentrated on and drawn to our attention with varying emphasis as fashions changed. We have been led to fasten our gaze upon a people's history and its highlights in divine choice and deliverance, epiphany and covenant, entry into the Land and expulsion from it—themes accentuated in Torah and Prophets, meditated and moralized on and declaimed by seers and spokesmen, by Deuteronomist and Chronicler. In no way was the viewpoint of a more recent moralist shared, that "the proper study of mankind is man."

So it involved a grinding of gears for scholars and other readers of the Bible to move off this mighty stage with its heroic and often tragic figures and to spend time with a character pondering down-to-earth questions about life in this banal setting and a God equally interested in it.

> What is man that you should make so much of him,
> subjecting him to your scrutiny,
> that morning after morning you should examine him
> and at every instant test him?
> Will you never take your eyes off me
> long enough for me to swallow my spittle?[1]

We can appreciate, while regretting, the dismay of a great biblical scholar discovering as "an astonishing fact" that "Wisdom has to do with man . . . , never the people as the elect of Yahweh."[2] Nourished on a shrunken canon and reading Wisdom only to the extent of Proverbs and Ecclesiastes, he could take as his first principle that "the faith of the Old Testament has its origins in the fundamental fact that God encountered Israel in the midst of history." An elevating and inspiring if shortsighted summation of the whole Bible: how reconcile it with the navel-gazing of (an equally shortsighted) Qoheleth?

> There is an evil that I have seen under the sun, and it lies heavy upon humankind: those to whom God gives wealth, possessions, and honor, so that they lack nothing of all that they desire, yet God does not enable them to enjoy these things, but a stranger enjoys them. This is vanity; it is a grievous ill (6:1-2).

Jesus likewise is happy to focus on slaves swindling masters, farmers sowing seed, women sweeping and searching for lost coins; he is not constantly harking back to God's great deeds in his people's salvation history.

A Concern with Human Nature

There is no doubt that Wisdom in the Bible has a human face. Since it is the Word of God we meet in those pages, this should hardly be a scandalous discovery; we are happy to accommodate within our Shakespearean corpus Lear and Bottom both, Falstaff and Juliet, so why in reading the Scriptures take fright at a dyspeptic pessimist pondering the limitations of old age, as Qoheleth does in that beautifully human chapter 12? We find other scholars who are prepared to accept that Wisdom is "anthropocentric" but who defensively insist also that "the claim of humanism be rejected."[3] What is wrong with finding humanists among biblical composers? Theirs is not a secular humanism, as we shall discuss further in

chapter 9; they are simply fascinated with the way human beings behave in a world of God's making. As we noted before,
the sages are prepared to admit the limitations of human wisdom because they recognize a pervasive divine Wisdom in the
scheme of things.[4]

At its most basic level, sapiential concern is with human
nature and the human condition. Umpteen of the ancient
proverbial encapsulations of human experience dwell on the
strengths and weaknesses of humanity.

> The heart knows its own bitterness,
> and no stranger shares its joy.

> The poor are disliked even by their neighbors,
> but the rich have many friends.

> The light of the eyes rejoices the heart,
> and good news refreshes the body.

> Pride goes before destruction,
> and a haughty spirit before a fall.

> A friend loves at all times,
> and kinsfolk are born to share adversity.

> A person's attire and hearty laughter,
> and the way he walks, show what he is.[5]

The Wisdom of many cultures ancient and modern medi-
ates such reflections upon human nature. Human proclivity to
evil and injustice predictably receives heavier accent.

> Again I saw all the oppressions that are practiced under the sun.
> Look, the tears of the oppressed—with no one to comfort them!
> On the side of their oppressors there was power—with no one to
> comfort them. And I thought the dead, who have already died,
> more fortunate than the living, who are still alive; but better than
> both is the one who has not yet been, and has not seen the evil
> deeds that are done under the sun.[6]

In similar vein is *A Dispute over Suicide* from the Egypt of the
end of the third millennium:

> To whom can I speak today?
>> One's fellows are evil;
>> The friends of today do not love.
> To whom can I speak today?
>> Hearts are rapacious:
>> Every man seizes his fellow's goods.
> To whom can I speak today?
>> The gentle man has perished,
>> But the violent man has access to everybody.
> To whom can I speak today?
>> Men are contented with evil;
>> Goodness is rejected everywhere.[7]

There is no doubt, too, that meditation on the human condition, especially one's own particular distress real or imagined, can produce the most intensely emotive statement, whether in Shakespeare or the Bible or ancient extrabiblical literature. This strengthens the claim of Wisdom to a human face beyond merely historical or legislative material, where the fate of a people or a divine epiphany, though moving, is also more remote. We cannot fail to be moved by the anguish of Job in the throes of personal distress; with the skill of a talented artist such human self-analysis makes for powerful expression.

> Why is light given to one in misery,
>> and life to the bitter in soul,
> who long for death, but it does not come,
>> and dig for it more than for hidden treasures;
> who rejoice exceedingly,
>> and are glad when they find the grave?
> Why is light given to one who cannot see the way,
>> whom God has fenced in?
> For my sighing comes like my bread,
>> and my groanings are poured out like water (Job 3:20-24).

Toil and Trade

Sages in all cultures ply their craft by proceeding from this insight into human nature to observe and prescribe appropriate behavior. Shakespeare's Polonius comes from a long line of well-meaning parents, counselors, scribes, secretarial assist-ants, viziers, even kings, who turned their hand to advising the young, the ignorant, the less competent, in the ways to behave in various contexts and occasions. Egypt and Mesopo-tamia had a large body of such didactic material amassed well before Israel's sages, the sect of Qumran, Jesus and his disciples, and the gnostic philosophers found the need of providing their ad-herents with similar instruction. We are indebted today to compilers like Pritchard and Lambert for making it as readily available to us as it was unlikely to have been within reach of biblical sages to adopt verbatim.

> Pay attention, my friend, understand my clever ideas,
> Heed my carefully chosen words.
> People extol the word of a strong man who has learned to kill
> But bring down the powerless who has done no wrong.
> They confirm the position of the wicked for whom what should
>   be an abomination is considered right
> Yet drive off the honest man who heeds the will of his god.
> They fill the storehouse of the oppressor with gold,
> But empty the larder of the beggar of its provisions.[8]

This Akkadian commentary on human behavior from *The Babylonian Theodicy* contemporary with Israel's early monarchy testifies to the age-old sapiential practice. It is akin to Qoheleth's laments of the oppression of the poor (5:8), if not equally confi-dent that in the end a divine Wisdom sets all to rights. It recalls the moral analysis of the host of sages contributing to Proverbs who touch on laziness (Prov 12:27; 13:4) and intemperance (23:20-21, 29ff.), gossiping (11:13; 20:19) and use of false bal-ances (11:1; 20:10) but who are equally observant of generosity (11:25) and diplomacy (15:1) and the relations between parents and children (15:5, 10-20; 17:21, 25; 19:26; 22:6)—a litany that Ben Sira parallels single-handedly. The way people behave is an inexhaustible source of commentary for the sages, if thought by some to be unbecoming to the Bible's operatic stage. Thankfully, Shakespeare—no mean sage himself—was not of that mind.

Correlatively, human skills are of interest to Wisdom: parenting and a provident spirit, control of tongue and temper, the banality of good table manners and the loftiness of kingship. William McKane, as we noted in the previous chapter, drew some criticism for his emphasis on the political skills of "old wisdom"; for him *binah,* "understanding," is a synonym for "wisdom" and can be translated "craftsmanship."[9] He could find support from more ancient Oriental sapiential composition, in which political skills are to the fore, like this instruction of Ptah-hotep, vizier to King Izezi of the Fifth Dynasty in Egypt around the middle of the third millennium:

> If thou art a leader commanding the affairs of the multitude, seek out for thyself every beneficial deed, until it may be that thy own affairs are without wrong. Justice is great, and its appropriateness is lasting; it has not been disturbed since the time of him who made it, whereas there is punishment for him who passes over its laws. It is the right path before him who knows nothing. Wrongdoing has never brought its undertaking into port. [10]

Do Wisdom's skills reach to the interpretation of dreams, in the manner of the two Josephs (in both Testaments) and Daniel? Or do those skills bring us into another climate, that of apocalyptic? We have noted above in chapter 1 that there is disagreement as to the extent of biblical Wisdom, for instance, whether the Joseph narrative belongs to it. On the face of it, considering the charged atmosphere of apocalyptic and the fact that 1 Kings confines Solomon's sapiential skills to proverbs and songs and analogies from nature, it seems better to leave dreams to the seers (even if Second Isaiah associated them with Babylon's sages).[11] Jesus the sage likewise changes roles in his apocalyptic discourses, where the tone palpably goes up several notches.[12]

A Universal Outlook

One of the most appealing aspects of Wisdom's human face and one of its great theological strengths is its universalism, and we have repeatedly found irony in the fact that this strength was counted a weakness by those in other ages, who were encouraged to see it as marginal, "peripheral,"[13] to the Bible's message (conceived inadequately). It is worth, if only as a lesson for ourselves, quoting G. Ernest Wright again: "The difficulty of the wisdom movement was that its theological base and interest were too narrowly fixed";[14] scholarship can be perverse and ignore the evidence. The contrary, of course, is true; Wisdom looks at *all* people, and in their most universal, basic categories of good and evil—not Jew or Gentile, not focusing on one racial group chosen "out of all the peoples" (Exod 19:5)—though, as we shall see below, Sirach[15] and Baruch and even the Wisdom of Solomon will want to insist that the Jewish people have been particularly blessed in the gift of wisdom. Jesus will not be concerned to harp on this qualification.

So the sages study generic human behavior—of parents and children (women and men?), of honest and dishonest, of peasants and princes, of lazy and diligent. Proverbs and New Testament parables are about all these types of people, who can be found the world over. Not all the Bible shares this viewpoint; the Book of Jonah is written (by a sage?) to suggest to Judaism that prophets could take the wider view and lose some of their prejudices, as Paul later has to constantly remind his Jewish listeners that they have been freed from such constraints. Not all other Jewish and Christian literature responds to this sapiential universalism. The Qumran community will transform the sages' basic categories into "children of light" and "children of darkness" on the basis of adherence to their own rigid code and creed, as *The Community Rule* reveals. Only snatches of intertestamental literature show an opening to a wider view.[16] *The Gospel of Thomas*, *The Hymn of the Pearl*, and gnostic composition generally will take Jesus' universal invitation in the Beatitudes and confine it to those who have achieved or been granted "self-acquaintance,"[17] *gnosis*.

So we have much to be grateful for in Wisdom's human face. It is a testimony to the irrepressibility of the human spirit that thinkers and composers could slip the limitations of their cultural, racial, and religious conditioning and ruminate in terms of humanity living under the providence of an all-loving God—an admirable anthropology. It has much to say to readers in any age of the danger of accepting a narrow, discriminatory view of the offer of life. The implications of such a partial reading of the Jewish and Christian Scriptures many of us have had to live through and lament. Thank God for the sages.

Notes

1. Job 7:17-19 *(JB)*.

2. W. Zimmerli, "The Place and Limit of the Wisdom in the Framework of the Old Testament Theology," *SJT* 17 (1964) 146–47.

3. Cf. Crenshaw, "Wisdom in the OT," *IDB* 954, and "Method in Determining Wisdom Influence upon 'Historical' Literature," *Studies in Ancient Israelite Wisdom*, 483.

4. See ch. 1, n. 9.

5. Prov 14:10; 14:20; 15:30; 16:18; 17:17; Sir 19:30.

6. Eccl 4:1-3; cf. Job 24:3-12.

7. J. B. Pritchard, ed., *Ancient Near Eastern Texts Relating to the Old Testament*, 3rd ed. (Princeton: Princeton Univ. Press, 1969) 405.

8. *ANET* 602.

9. "The wisdom literature is, for the most part, a product not of full-time men of letters and academics, but of men of affairs in high places of state, and the literature in some of its forms bears the marks of its close association with those who exercise the skills of statecraft" (*Prophets and Wise Men*, 44).

10. ANET 412. McKane would find Ptah-hotep's mellowness falling short of the "pragmatic, unethical, irreligious" sages of Israel's "old wisdom" (*Prophets and Wise Men*, 47).

11. Isa 47:10-13. In ch. 5 we shall have to suspect the sapiential credentials of Job's friends when they claim the authority of dreams for their position.

12. Cf. Matt 24–25.

13. John Bright: see above, ch. 1, n. 32.

14. See ch. 1, n. 31.

15. Ben Sira, though, is divided in his loyalties. As a sage he can recast the Sinai story to include all peoples in covenant (17:11-14); as true

Israelite he eventually confines wisdom to one people (17:17; cf. 33:10-12).

16. Cf. *1 Enoch* 48: "[The Son of Man] will be the light of the nations, and he will be the hope of those who grieve in their hearts" (H.F.D. Sparks, *The Apocryphal Old Testament* [Oxford: Clarendon, 1984] 229); *The Testament of Levi* 14: "What will all the Gentiles do, . . . for whose sake the light of the law was given?" (Sparks, 533–34).

17. Bentley Layton's consistent translation of the term in his collection (*The Gnostic Scriptures*, London: SCM, 1987).

3

The Social Face of Wisdom

Typical of Wisdom and, within the Bible, peculiar to it is a concentration on the human condition. This led to its being emarginated from the mainstream of biblical scholarship, as we have also noted. It is not that Law and Prophets are uninterested in human behavior; they are, of course, very moral documents, as Ben Sira's grandson acknowledged. Jewish scholars remind us to define Torah adequately, despite the Septuagint's settling for *nomos;* better, in Jacob Neusner's words, "the whole body of belief, doctrine, practice, patterns of piety and behaviour, and moral and intellectual commitments that constitute the Judaic version of reality."[1] Some, for that reason, see in torah material a sapiential character (Ben Sira would agree: 39:1-5) and trace the influence of the sages even on the apodictic laws of the Decalogue.[2]

Yet there is evident in Torah and Prophets a different approach to the issues of social conduct. Perhaps we can be satisfied with Zimmerli's summary of the basis of that approach —"the fundamental fact that God encountered Israel in the midst of history."[3] Covenant prescriptions about the proper behavior of a people under treaty, which is how both these bodies of moral teaching present social intercourse, is far from the way the sages address the question of how people generally do and should behave toward one another. Moving boundary stones[4] or taking bribes[5] is regrettable social conduct, no matter whether one's God has spoken from Sinai or not. The sages are not concerned with the covenant fidelity of David or Ahaz or the whole people of northern or southern kingdoms and the fate that awaits them. The "Words of the Wise" and the Deuteronomistic history approach morality from different standpoints; the former finds ready parallels instead in Egyptians Ani and Amen-em-Opet, in the Akkadian *Ludlul Bel Nemeqi,* and even in the New Testament's James.

Universal Social Concerns

> One who augments wealth by exorbitant interest
> > gathers it for another who is kind to the poor.
> Do not laugh at a blind man nor tease a dwarf
> > nor injure the affairs of the lame.
> Thou shouldst not sit when another who is older than thou is standing,
> > or one who has been raised higher in his rank.
> Like a war club, a sword, or a sharp arrow
> > is one who bears false witness against a neighbour.
> Let your speech always be gracious, seasoned with salt,
> > so that you may know how you ought to answer everyone.
> To guarantee loans for a stranger brings trouble,
> > but there is safety in refusing to do so.
> Through sloth the roof sinks in,
> > and through indolence the house leaks.
> The senseless have vain and false hopes,
> > and dreams give wings to fools.[6]

We might have difficulty tracing the precise source of each of these maxims about social intercourse relevant the world over —about taking loans and charging excessive interest, employing false weights, abusing the tongue and giving false witness, about laziness and industry. But they are clearly sapiential in character and their moral standpoint identifiably distinct from classic Torah or Prophets—except where these simply incorporate age-old traditional advice. We shall examine sapiential morality in chapter 6.

We have no difficulty, at any rate, in accepting that Wisdom has a social face. It is unashamedly interested in observing and advising on human converse, the dealings of people everywhere—hence the disappearance of racially and culturally distinctive features in the above miscellany. For this reason scholars can speak of the "international" character of Wisdom. There is further support for that tag: Solomon in the encomium in 1 Kings is compared favorably with Canaanite sages; the Book of Proverbs closes with some blocks of foreign Wisdom; the prophets also speak (generally unfavorably) of sages from Babylon and Edom; Israel's Wisdom shows undoubted influence of—if not slavish dependence on—Egyptian, Canaanite, and Phoenician models.[7]

What is not international about Wisdom, however, or national either for that matter, is its lack of interest in relationships at the level of the major political forces of the day—in a word, international politics. And this is so despite the fact that the precise tone of a particular sapiential composition owes something to political developments. The radicalism that Qoheleth and the Book of Job bring to traditional sapiential morality is quite likely due to the disillusionment arising from the trauma of the Exile; the world has fallen apart and traditional patterns with it. Yet these sages never advert to such developments. To some commentators this silence is a defect; to others "it is precisely the absence of this national frame of reference that lends to biblical wisdom its great importance."[8]

The Sages and Politics

This is not to say the sages were utterly apolitical. The paradigmatic association of Wisdom with Solomon would suggest otherwise, as does the frequent reference to kingly behavior in proverbial material.[9] We have mentioned above the suggestion of the court as one locus of Wisdom schools. McKane and Von Rad are at one in seeing these schools in "old wisdom" as discharging the purpose of forming government officials in administrative skills; they differ as to whether any religious or ethical element characterized this formation.[10] Certainly there was precedent in Egyptian Wisdom for political critique; *The Protests of the Eloquent Peasant* from the late third millennium powerfully and at length highlights abuse of power by corrupt officials.[11] Old and New Testament sages, however, do not seem to take the matter so seriously in merely political terms. If the Book of Job is taken less as speculative theology than as criticism of the world order,[12] it appeals not to politicians but to social systems to redress social imbalance. The socially sensitive epistle of James likewise does not look to politicians for relief of distress. Awareness of these social concerns is obviously germane to Wisdom.

Yet for all its human interest and social sensitivity, Wisdom —even but not solely biblical Wisdom—is notoriously insensitive when it comes to expressing its attitude toward women. Qoheleth, admittedly dyspeptic in the best of times, despairs of finding anything good to say about them. "I found more bitter than death the woman who is a trap, whose heart is snares and nets, whose hands are fetters; one who pleases God escapes her, but the sinner is taken by her. . . . One man among a thousand I found, but a woman among all these I have not found" (7:26, 28).[13] Like Qoheleth and Ben Sira,[14] the authors of Proverbs so often[15] depict the male as ever prey to the "loose woman," not to mention the frequently appearing "adulteress"[16] and numerous sardonic remarks about the "contentious woman."[17] The improbability of this aspect of social relations in contemporary Oriental society makes one wonder about the basis of the widespread statement of the predatory female and the witless male, which is argued perversely:

> Better is the wickedness of a man than a woman who does good;
> it is woman who brings shame and disgrace (Sir 42:14).[18]

Job's wife, who does not merit a mention in the verse drama, is dismissed as a foolish woman in the prose,[19] where, moreover, she does not figure in the final restoration of family fortunes.

The Relation of the Sexes

The Bible has no monopoly on this obviously stereotypical presentation of the relation of the sexes. Many centuries earlier in Egypt *The Instruction of Ani* was warning the young male, "Be on thy guard against a woman from abroad . . . when she waits to ensnare thee."[20] Akkadian Wisdom could maintain in *A Dialogue of Pessimism* that "a woman is a pitfall, a hole, a ditch, a woman is a sharp iron dagger that slits a man's throat,"[21] and the *Counsels of Wisdom* offers advice on a man's relations with slave girls and prostitutes—not so much to give them a wide berth as to keep them from gaining the upper hand.[22] It is clearly lectures on social converse, not moral values, we are getting—"manners before morals," in Oscar Wilde's terms—and the theme is well entrenched.

So well entrenched, of course, that it survives the Old Testament to appear in intertestamental literature, at Qumran, and in places in the New Testament; one thinks of the Pauline household codes, for instance. It is not for us here to remark on the continuity of this well-rehearsed theme into Christian or Jewish theology and praxis until more recent times. We should, however, point to the theme's appearance in other influential literature of the biblical period. *The Testaments of the Twelve Patriarchs* was long regarded as a Pharisaic composition of late Old Testament times and as such "became firmly established as an essential part of the 'background reading' required of all students of New Testament theology and ethics"—until, that is, a much later date of composition was recently proved.[23] This influential, basically Christian work incorporates the well-worn position on the relation of the sexes: "Women are evil, my children: because they have no power or strength to stand up against man, they use wiles and try to ensnare him by their charms; and man, whom woman cannot subdue by strength, she subdues by guile."[24]

Pride of place, however, in this distortion of the nature and position of women in religious literature of the biblical period must go to the dualistic attitude of the gnostics, expressed quintessentially in the final saying of *The Gospel of Thomas:*

> Simon Peter said to them, "Mary should leave us, for females are not worthy of life." Jesus said, "See, I am going to attract her to make her male so that she too might become a living spirit that resembles you males. For every female (element) that makes itself male will enter the kingdom of heaven."[25]

The sexism, even misogyny, we find in Wisdom, therefore, occurs in a wide literary context that is doubtless affected by social attitudes in a range of cultures over the lengthy period of some millennia. We are obviously dealing with a literary stereotype arising from a social stereotype that has clearly influenced religion, theology, and practice. The sages have not been sage enough or courageous enough to resist the societal pressure. Can we say that all those we have on record are male? Should an exception be made for "The words of King Lemuel. An oracle that his mother taught him" in Proverbs 31, complete with its own warning against women in the poem that follows on the good, or useful, wife?[26]

Woman Wisdom: An Anomaly

That final poem in Proverbs, if also stereotypical, is anomalous in spending some time on a positive though utilitarian portrait of a woman. For Kathleen O'Connor[27] and others, however, it is no typical woman described here but rather a portrait of "the strong woman," to be identified with "the Wisdom Woman" as opposed to "the Strange Woman," those male stereotypes of womanhood depicted earlier. No real woman in ancient Israel, observes O'Connor, held such a high place in family, society, or economy as the poem imagines. We are instead being shown what life is like once one has chosen to live with the Wisdom Woman.

Be that as it may in Proverbs 31, the remarkable anomaly in this matter of Wisdom's stance on the relation of the sexes is the personification or hypostatization of wisdom[28] as a woman,

"Lady Wisdom" or "Woman Wisdom,"[29] that occurs at several places in biblical and extrabiblical Wisdom.

The passage in Proverbs 8, its replica in Sirach 24[30] and Wisdom of Solomon 7:22ff., are best known for this presentation of wisdom, but we need to recall also Proverbs 1:20-33; 3:13-18; 4:5-9 as well as Sirach 51:13-32 (a text found as well at Qumran embedded in the Psalms scroll). Qumran also offers us a noncanonical psalm, the Syriac Psalm II, classed by Vermes as "a sapiential hymn," in which wisdom is given by the Lord and made known to man:

> From the doors of the righteous her voice is heard, and from the
> congregation of the devout her song.[31]

While this psalm may be too ancient to be the work of the Qumran sect, what does seem to come from them is a recently published set of beatitudes[32] akin to those in the Gospels and the lesser-known Old Testament ones like Sirach 25:7-10 and another (in which wisdom is again presented as a person, with a home of her own outside which the virtuous man camps), Sirach 14:20-27. Beatitudes, Benedict Viviano says in his commentary, are a (still further) sapiential genre dealing with the living of the good life; and in this Qumranic set wisdom personified is presented to the good person as a proper object of search:

> Blessed is he who seeks her with pure hands
>   and who does not go after her with a deceitful heart.

Wisdom in person appears also in intertestamental literature and the New Testament. In *The Words of Ahiqar*, which gained wide currency in Jewish and Christian circles following its composition possibly in northern Syria around the sixth century, she appears in a polytheistic heavenly court:

> To gods also she is dear. For all time the kingdom is hers. In heaven
> is she established, for the lord of the holy ones has exalted her.[33]

In *The Odes of Solomon* in the Christian era she appears in a fashion modeled on Proverbs 8 (7:7ff.; 11:5ff.); when she speaks, it is in gnostic terms with an accent on truth and knowledge (8:8-21). In our next chapter we shall see the author of *1 Enoch* reworking the key texts about Woman Wisdom in Proverbs and Sirach to avoid her having to come into contact with this world.

Wisdom Hypostatized?

It is certainly an anomaly we are presented with in this dignified presentation of Woman Wisdom, so prevalent in ancient religious literature where the role and value of womankind is—sometimes in the same breath—equally widely demeaned. Even if merely a figure of speech is involved, wisdom personified as an attractive, caring woman, the disparity is hard to accommodate. Yet can these numerous passages be understood simply as a figure of speech? Are we encouraged to think in terms of hypostatization, wisdom as a (divine) person/hypostasis? Polytheistic cultures would have little difficulty including another figure in their theogonies, but Jewish religion and theology find it abhorrent.

So the passage in the Hebrew Scriptures about the figure of Woman Wisdom, who speaks of herself in relation to God and creation in Proverbs 8 (which seems to be a reference for later such biblical and apocryphal passages), assumes a particular importance. Bruce Vawter has argued with authority that the Hebrew verb *qana* in 8:22 does not justify translation as "the Lord created me" but "the Lord acquired me"; he adds that "wisdom appears here as a being existing before all created things, not a creature, therefore, but a prior *[sic]* to creation, which was attainable and attained by God, who then concurred with it in the creation and ordering of the universe."[34] So some commentators speak easily of hypostatization or interchangeability of the two terms;[35] others point out that more is involved in Woman Wisdom than other biblical personifications like the "Arm of Yahweh," or the "Righteousness which goes before Yahweh."[36] In two 1990 publications Roland Murphy shows a common indecision, insisting that only personification is involved,[37] then doubting whether "'personification' does justice to the figure of Wisdom" on the grounds that "the very origins and the authority of Wisdom suggest more than a personified order of creation. Wisdom is somehow identified with the Lord." Yet for Murphy "hypostasis" carries too much philosophical baggage.[38]

The New Testament, of course, has no reservations about exploiting the ambiguous richness of this background in its task of introducing the Word preexistent and incarnate. Paul and his disciples, wrestling with Jewish tendencies to identify wisdom with Torah and wanting also to bring the cosmos into considerations of universal salvation, found in hymns like that absorbed into Colossians 1:15ff. a terminology and sapiential breadth of background well suited as a context for evaluating the origins and mission of Jesus.[39] Evangelists like Matthew and John could see Jesus as Woman Wisdom incarnate,[40] recognizable by her deeds,[41] inviting in sapiential terms all to come to gain knowledge of divine things[42] and relief.[43] Later, however, in the gnostic creation myth Wisdom, *Sophia*, will lose any attractiveness on account of her reprehensible role in material creation.[44]

For us, in our study of the social face of Wisdom and the relation of the sexes in particular, the question is more basic still: Why does biblical Wisdom, with its poor track record in this area, speak of wisdom as a woman at all? Is it simply a matter of grammatical gender, the fact that "wisdom" in Hebrew (and Greek) is feminine? Or is there an attempt to offset attention in Israel to the goddess of fertility, Astarte?[45] Or are we seeing influence of figures from Egyptian pantheons, like Ma'at and Ishtar and Isis?[46] Or should we look instead to Canaanite mythology, now that the tide has turned and become "eblaïtique"?[47]

We are left with this anomaly in considering Wisdom's social face. It is particularly intriguing in our time when we respond negatively to the less appealing features of a body of literature that takes an interest in the way people relate to one another. Perhaps we have to remind ourselves, as Paul did in his time and Zophar before him, that Wisdom is multifaceted, *polypoikilos.* Not every face may be clear and attractive.

Notes

1. *Judaism in the Beginnings of Christianity* (Philadelphia: Fortress, 1984) 12.

2. Cf. E. Nielsen, *The Ten Commandments in a New Perspective: A Traditio-historical Approach* (1965), English trans. (Studies in Biblical Theology, 2nd Series, 7, London: SCM, 1968) 56–57, 64, 75–77, 116–18, 124.

3. "The Place and Limit of the Wisdom in the Framework of the Old Testament Theology," *SJT* 17 (1964) 147.

4. Cf. Prov 22:28; 23:10.

5. Cf. Prov 17:8, 23; 21:14.

6. A miscellany of social advice from Prov 28:8; *The Instruction of Amen-em-Opet* 24:10 (*ANET* 424); *The Instruction of Ani* (*ANET* 420); Prov 25:18; Col 4:6; Prov 11:15; Eccl 10:18; Sir 34:1.

7. See ch. 1, n. 10.

8. R. E. Clements, *Wisdom for a Changing World,* 23.

9. Clements asks the question of why such reference to the monarchy continued into postexilic Wisdom and concludes: "Cosmic order, as taught in the tradition of wisdom, supported the principle of kingship, even that of a foreign ruler such as Cyrus!" (ibid., 72).

10. See the assessment of the arguments by B. S. Childs, *Biblical Theology of the Old and New Testaments* (Minneapolis: Fortress, 1992) 188–89.

11. *ANET* 407–10.

12. As does W. Brueggemann, "Theodicy in a Social Dimension," *JSOT* 33 (1985) 3–25.

13. For some commentators, however, like Roland Murphy and Addison G. Wright, Qoheleth is here simply reflecting current platitudes about women, which in v. 29 he puts to one side in concluding, "See, this alone I found, that God made human beings straightforward, but they have devised many schemes." For Murphy, "Qoheleth would be denying the truth of a saying that attempted to make a distinction between man and woman" ("On translating Ecclesiastes," *CBQ* 53, no. 4 [1991] 574).

14. Sir 9:2-9; 25:16-26; 26:5-11; 42:9-14. Ben Sira's lectures on adultery are directed to the wife (23:22-27), not the husband.

15. Cf. Prov 2:16-19; 5:3; 6:24; 7:5; 9:13; 22:14. In Cave 4 at Qumran was discovered a poem Vermes (*The Dead Sea Scrolls in English*, . 3rd ed, [Harmondsworth: Penguin, 1988] 240–41) entitled "The Seductress" on this same theme, perhaps inspired by Proverbs and intent on developing it further. As with other materials found on site, a question may be raised as to whether it is the work of the residents.

16. Cf. Prov 23:27-28; 30:20.

17. Cf. Prov 21:9, 19; 25:24; 27:15-16.

18. The *NAB*'s version, "Better a man's harshness than a woman's indulgence, and a frightened daughter than any disgrace" and its textual notes keeping the focus of vv. 9-14 on "A father's care for his daughter" put a different complexion on what otherwise appears as unmitigated misogynism. (I am grateful to Roland Murphy, who concurs with the *NAB*, for drawing my attention to this.)

19. Job 2:10.

20. *ANET* 420.

21. *ANET* 601.

22. *ANET* 595.

23. H.F.D. Sparks, *The Apocryphal Old Testament*, 509.

24. *The Testament of Reuben* 5 (Sparks, 519).

25. Layton, *The Gnostic Scriptures*, 399. St Augustine (if David Jasper of Glasgow University is to be believed, no reference supplied) concurred: in the resurrection of the body, "virgins who remain virgins may, if they are lucky, become male" (reported in *The Tablet* [June 11, 1994] 738).

26. Cf. Carole R. Fontaine, "Proverbs," *The Women's Bible Commentary*, ed. C. Newsom and S. Ringe (London: SPCK, 1992) 146: "As always in male-centered scripture, the positive and negative roles of women are viewed primarily from the perspective of what they provide for the men involved. Nowhere does one hear the sages condemn a society that forced some women into prostitution; one hears only about the havoc such women can wreak on a young man's promising career. This is not unique to Israelite wisdom but is typical of the international tradition as well."

27. *The Wisdom Literature* (Message of Biblical Spirituality 5, Wilmington: Glazier, 1988) 77.

28. It is perhaps appropriate to see the quality of wisdom, not the body of material we know as Wisdom and its peculiar perspective, that

is being viewed (if only metaphorically) as a woman. It is but one face of the whole we encounter here. So lower case is in order.

29. Feminist commentators, like Carole Fontaine ("Proverbs"), predictably prefer the latter term.

30. Immediately following the diatribe against a woman's adultery (23:22-27)!

31. *The Dead Sea Scrolls in English*, 209–10. Vermes adds that the psalm itself is not definitely sectarian.

32. Cf. B. T. Viviano, "Beatitudes Found among Dead Sea Scrolls," *Biblical Archeology Review* 18, no. 6 (1992) 53–55, 66.

33. *ANET* 429.

34. "Prov 8:22: Wisdom and Creation," *JBL* 99 (1980) 207.

35. Crenshaw, "Prolegomenon," 25.

36. Rankin, *Israel's Wisdom Literature*, 224.

37. "Introduction to Wisdom Literature," *NJBC* 450.

38. *The Tree of Life*, 133, 138. A systematic theologian like Paul Tillich has no such difficulties with speaking of Wisdom (as of Word and Glory) as one of those "hypostatized qualities or functions of God," "Christianity Judging Itself in the Light of Its Encounter with the World Religions," *Christianity and Other Religions*, ed. J. Hick and B. Hebblethwaite (London: Fount, 1980) 113.

39. See my "Mystery of Christ: Clue to Paul's Thinking on Wisdom," *The Heythrop Journal* 25 (1984) 475–83. J.D.G. Dunn considers Paul's use of Wisdom motifs in *Christology in the Making* (London: SCM, 1980) 176–212—a treatment that is marred by an a priori reluctance to see any reference to preexistence in Pauline texts.

40. "The Q tradition has combined the image of Jesus as eschatological prophet with that of Jesus as Wisdom's spokesperson." P. Perkins and R. Fuller, *Who Is This Christ? Gospel Christology and Contemporary Faith* (Philadelphia: Fortress, 1983) 55.

41. Matt 11:19, where Matthew adapts the less-pointed reference to Jesus from *Q* found at Luke 7:35.

42. John 6:35, 51ff.; 4:13-14. See R. E. Brown, "Wisdom Motifs," *The Gospel According to John I–XII*, Anchor Bible (Garden City: Doubleday, 1966) 29:cxxii–cxxvii.

43. Matt 11:25-27; Luke 10:21-22.

44. Cf. Layton, *The Gnostic Scriptures*, 12–18.

45. Murphy, *Introduction to the Wisdom Literature of the Old Testament*, 50.

46. Crenshaw, "Wisdom in the OT," *IDB* 956; Murphy, *Introduction to the Wisdom Literature of the Old Testament,* 51; "Wisdom and Creation," *JBL* 104 (1985) 5.

47. Dahood, "Eblaite and Biblical Hebrew," 22.

4

Wisdom's Cosmic Dimension

One of Wisdom's many faces is firmly directed to the real world—not only of people but also of the created universe. The sages have an interest in and an affinity with natural phenomena in the way other bodies of religious literature find them largely irrelevant. It is a question again of which stage is the scene of the action: the small stage of grand opera where heroic figures work out national tragedies or the sweeping if low-key scenario of mundane realities. Ben Sira could survey the whole panoply of Israel's heroes, could constantly urge meditation on the Law of the Lord, but as a true if atypically pious sage he could also take account of the world where ordinary people live their ordinary lives:

> Hard work was created for everyone,
> > and a heavy yoke is laid on the children of Adam.
> Cattle and orchards make one prosperous,
> > but a blameless wife is accounted better than either (40:1, 19b).[1]

Contact with the Real World

In fact, it is particularly their contact with and appreciation of the real world made by the Creator that furnishes the sages, Jesus included, with their true credentials. In face of this, the

inadequacy of those one-liners defining Wisdom shows up—
the "didactic literature" of Von Rad, others' "hagiography," "ra-
tiocination."[2] In our time Wisdom has come to be esteemed
for this cosmic awareness; Von Rad himself, who, though in
Wisdom in Israel moving positively from his earlier disparage-
ment of Wisdom did not succeed in grasping its true nature,
underwent something of a conversion in reading Sirach 42:21-
25 and gasped with astonished admiration: "What a view of
the world this is! . . . How small a step it was from knowledge
to adoration!"[3] How could he not have responded with like appreciation to Job and parts of Proverbs and Ecclesiastes where
this cosmic dimension appears? Did his view of Wisdom as didactic literature condition him to look only for pedestrian lectures on morality and ignore Wisdom's other faces? He could
have read again what his beloved Deuteronomist thinks constitutes Solomon's claim to the status of a sage.

The Deuteronomist, in fact, and other shapers of Israel's
historical traditions proved a stumbling block for Von Rad and
others in appreciating this dimension of biblical Wisdom. If
one is constantly focusing on "a process of history which is
formed by the word of Jahweh continually intervening in
judgement and salvation and directed towards a fulfilment,"[4]
one will find an irritating irrelevance any such comment as
Qoheleth's: "The fate of humans and the fate of animals is the
same; as one dies, so dies the other. They all have the same
breath, and humans have no advantage over the animals; for all
is vanity. All go to one place; all are from the dust, and all turn
to dust again" (Eccl 3:19-20). It is not passages like these that
move someone like Von Rad to admiration, and yet they are as
genuinely sapiential as the passage from Sirach. Even today,
when cosmologists and conservationists delight in discovering
the sages' interest in "creation," it is for those elevated surveys
of the work of God the creator rather than mundane details of
the world as created that takes their fancy.[5] To the former
alone they tend to apply the tag "theology of creation."

No Dualism in Wisdom

Yet both are aspects of this sapiential interest in created realities. Perhaps the word "cosmic" is misleading; "material" or "this-worldly" might be more appropriate. There is no immaterialist dualism in biblical Wisdom such as becomes apparent in some intertestamental works, gnostic compositions, and at places in the New Testament. In *1 Enoch*, where the author has in mind the figure of Wisdom in Proverbs and Sirach visiting and at home on earth, a necessary corrective is employed: "Wisdom found no place where she could dwell, and her dwelling was in heaven. Wisdom went out in order to dwell among the sons of men, but did not find a dwelling; wisdom returned to her place and took her place among the angels" (42). In heaven and among the angels is the place where we should live, suggests also the gnostic *Hymn of the Pearl,* in which the prince after a visit to earth peels off the sordid robe of his humanity.[6] For *The Odes of Solomon* this world is corrupt; we must leave it for a "new world" so as to find "incorruption" (33). The New Testament will have to insist (consistently?)[7] that this is not the way to envisage the Word incarnate.[8] At least the Jesus of the Synoptics shows no discomfort with this-worldly realities in both his life and his teaching.

No, the sages maintain, heaven and spirit are not the only relevant dimensions of the Creator's work, nor are judgment and salvation and history's fulfillment. The Ben Sira whose survey of the universe could excite Von Rad also surveys the lowly work of potter and smith, ploughman and scribe, and endorses the validity of their humdrum tasks:

> They do not sit in the judge's seat
>   nor do they understand the decisions of the courts;
> they cannot expound discipline or judgment,
>   and they are not found among the rulers.
> But they maintain the fabric of the world,
>   and their concern is for the exercise of their trade (38:33-34).

Lessons from Nature

So Qoheleth and Ben Sira, the authors of Proverbs and Job (less so The Wisdom of Solomon), and Jesus, too, have no problem with drawing from nature for their parabolic teaching. "A living dog is better than a dead lion,"[9] observes Qoheleth in urging an appreciation of existence. Job's chapter 28 teaches us of the inaccessibility and value of wisdom through sustained comparison with the mining of precious metals.[10] Proverbs is full of keen observation of the world:

> The beginning of strife is like letting out water;
>> so stop before the quarrel breaks out.
> As a door turns on its hinges,
>> so does a lazy person in bed (Prov 17:14; 26:14).[11]

The meaning of the *basileia* that Jesus mentions a hundred times is clarified by comparison with pearls of great price, treasures in fields, small seeds growing into great bushes.

We can learn not only from Torah and Prophets and the heroes they present but even from the animals, say the sages. Jesus directs us to the birds of the air, sparrows, foxes, hen and chickens. For an older teacher it is an ant:

> Go to the ant, you lazybones;
>> consider its ways, and be wise.
> Without having any chief
>> or officer or ruler,
> it prepares its food in summer,
>> and gathers its sustenance in harvest.
> How long will you lie there, O lazybones?
>> When will you rise from your sleep? (Prov 6:6-9).[12]

An Implicit Theology

There is, of course, implicit in this attention to material creation, Paul's *pasa ktisis*,[13] a profound theology despite the lack of explicit theologizing by the composers. The worldview of the sages, their vision of all that a generous Providence bestows and controls, extends to every single thing that human beings can observe. It certainly extends beyond a single people on the way to a fulfillment of their own devising, even if this earns Wisdom the scorn of the tradition historians. "What this wisdom teaching has to say only passes over into theology where the subject-matter contains some kind of pointer or reference to Jahweh, his activity, or what pleases or displeases him," they would claim; it was awaiting "a decided movement into the realm of theology."[14]

Not only does this verdict reflect a particular view of canon, as we have noted, but also a limited understanding of theology and its object. The God of legitimate theology surely does not have to be Israel's God, nor the beneficiaries solely one nation, or any nation; creation and the plan for it extend further—as Paul understood in speaking of the mystery of Christ (not simply the person of Jesus) extending to "all things, things in heaven and things on earth,"[15] and he employed *sophia* as a synonym for that comprehensive design. Other biblical composers, too, who point to the created universe when there is question of divine Wisdom (including the author of the verse *Job* and even "Agur son of Jakeh"), share this understanding of theology.

Creation Theology

So when tempted to give credit to some parts (only) of Wisdom for a "theology of creation," we should remember not to confine our attention only to such overt statements as

> The Lord by wisdom founded the earth;
> by understanding he established the heavens (Prov 3:19).

This is certainly a basic sapiential conviction. It underlies the divine response in Job (chs. 38–41) and its "pocket edition" (ch. 28) and is enunciated also at 9:5-10; 11:7-9; 12:7-9; 22:12; 37:14-24. Ben Sira begins with it at 1:1-3 and develops the theme at length at 42:15–43:33.[16] But we should see the same theology informing those other texts where an interest is taken in all aspects of material creation.

So the intention of commentators recognizing a "theology of creation" in Wisdom should be examined for adequacy. We can concede with Walther Zimmerli that "Wisdom thinks resolutely within the framework of a theology of creation";[17] but since his study is confined to Proverbs and Ecclesiastes, we have to wonder about the basis of his conclusion. With sounder claim to adequacy, A. M. Dubarle[18] and Luis Alonso Schökel have even detected the hand of sages in the second Genesis Creation account, where Adam himself is pictured as a sage, classifying and naming the animals, and where questions of the knowledge of good and evil and the origin of sin are raised.[19] We are reminded that Ben Sira retells the story of creation in his own sapiential way at 16:26–17:17 and again at 39:12-35.

Prophets and Sages on Creation

When a comparison is made between Wisdom accents on creation and a "theology of creation" in prophets like Deutero-Isaiah,[20] one has to wonder if the term is being used univocally. Certainly the prophet is reminiscent of the Book of Job and Agur son of Jakeh in assuring the exiles,

> Who has measured the waters in the hollow of his hand
> and marked off the heavens with a span,
> enclosed the dust of the earth in a measure,
> and weighed the mountains in scales
> and the hills in a balance? (Isa 40:12).

His interest, however, is not in created realities themselves but in the power Yahweh demonstrated in bringing them into being, a power he can demonstrate yet again in bringing the exiles out of slavery. That was not the intent of the author of Job, nor Agur's, nor Ben Sira's; they discern and admire divine Wisdom in the works of the Lord.

> All wisdom is from the Lord,
>> and with him it remains forever.
> The sand of the sea, the drops of rain,
>> and the days of eternity—who can count them? (Sir 1:1-2).

Not only that, but they take time to relish these natural beauties. Who but a sage could have composed that meditative study of old age that closes the Book of Ecclesiastes, from which the pathos emerges through a series of vivid natural images and symbols of fading vitality put together by someone with an affinity with nature:

> Remember your creator in the days of your youth, . . . before the sun and the light and the moon and the stars are darkened and the clouds return with the rain; . . . before the silver cord is snapped, and the golden bowl is broken, and the pitcher is broken at the fountain, and the wheel broken at the cistern, and the dust returns to the earth as it was, and the breath returns to God who gave it.[21]

It might also be said of the Jesus of the Synoptic Gospels that he is at home in the world of nature, as far as his teaching suggests; if Solomon-like in this, we are assured that a greater than Solomon can be seen at work in him, and evidence of this sapiential character of his is more extensive.

So in Wisdom's theology of creation we find a greater depth than is true of prophets like Second Isaiah and a more consistent interest and appreciation of the cosmos than emerges simply in the figure of wisdom hypostatized at a couple of isolated places in Proverbs and Sirach. As we said at the outset of this chapter, one of Wisdom's faces is firmly set in the direction of the real world; it declines to be swept away in a heady fervor to some other world, a refuge taken by apocalyptic. Why this steadiness of direction, especially when the rest of the Bible is largely uninterested?

Order in Creation

Should we see it as yet another influence of those more ancient literatures of Egypt and Mesopotamia, where Ma'at or

Marduk or some other divine principle of order is acknowledged as being in control, as in the Akkadian *Ludlul Bel Nemeqi?*[22] In the wake of the work of scholars of this mind like H. H. Schmid it can be said that "the concept of order is widely accepted in the current understanding of biblical wisdom."[23] Biblical texts such as Proverbs 8 could be adduced to support H. Gunkel's theory of *Chaoskampf,* since there we read of Yahweh creator drawing circles and setting limits (vv. 27, 29), thus eliminating chaos. In striving to find a "structure" for Old Testament Wisdom thinking, Zimmerli concludes that "for the wise man, the whole world arranges itself into a scale of values within which every entity has its place."[24]

Whatever accounts for insistence on order in creation that occurs in other works of the biblical period like *The Words of Ahiqar,*[25] *1 Enoch* 101, *The Testament of Naphtali* 3, *The Psalms of Solomon* 18,[26] there is no need in biblical Wisdom to have recourse to exotic explanations for the consistency of attention to created realities or their underlying theology. No need to look any further than the foxes and the birds of the air, as Jesus tells us, or the author of Job before him:

> Ask the animals, and they will teach you;
>> the birds of the air, and they will tell you;
> ask the plants of the earth, and they will teach you;
>> and the fish of the sea will declare to you.
> Who among all these does not know
>> that the hand of the Lord has done this? (12:7-9).

One thing the sages knew and delighted to ponder constantly, and that was the presence of divine Wisdom in all the world.

Notes

1. Admittedly, the stage of *The Wisdom of Solomon* could hardly be called low-key, generally.

2. See p. 5 above.

3. *Wisdom in Israel,* 306.

4. G. Von Rad, "The Deuteronomistic Theology of History in the Books of Kings," *Studies in Deuteronomy* (1948), English trans. (London: SCM, 1953) 91.

5. Matthew Fox, for instance, is inclined to be selective in this way in his (brief) examination of OT Wisdom in *The Coming of the Cosmic Christ*, 83–85, thus forfeiting a more adequate account in "Biblical Sources for Belief in the Cosmic Christ."

6. Wisdom 9:15 shows similar impatience with the human condition—a further index of its shaky claim to true Wisdom.

7. Jerome Neyrey notes in John "a series of recurring dualisms which dichotomize the cosmos into heaven/earth and spirit/flesh spheres," which then are replicated in the Gospel's Christology *(An Ideology of Revolt: John's Christology in Social-Science Perspective* [Philadelphia: Fortress, 1988] 155).

8. Cf. 1 John 4:2.

9. Eccl 9:4; cf. 1:6-7; 9:12; 11:3.

10. Cf. Job 5:7; 6:5; 8:11; 14:7-9, 11.

11. Cf. Prov 20:5, 15; 21:1, 19; 24:13; 25:11-14; 30:24-28. Also cf. Sir 3:30; 11:3; 13:1; 13:17-19; 24:13-17; 27:6; Wis 2:4; 4:4-5; 5:9-12.

12. Cf. Prov 7:22-23; Eccl 3:19.

13. Rom 8:22.

14. G. Von Rad, *Old Testament Theology* 1, 437, 440. In *Wisdom in Israel* Von Rad admits "a 'theologization' of wisdom" only at a late period with Proverbs 1–9, Job, Sirach (300, n. 16).

15. Cf. Eph 1:10. See my *Jesus and the Mystery of Christ* for development of this idea with emphasis on Paul and Wisdom and application of their theology to creation.

16. Not to mention the cryptic statement of divine creation in that work, possibly Jewish or Christian of the first or second century, *2 Enoch* 11:21: "And when I had finished everything, I commanded my wisdom to create man."

17. "The Place and Limit of the Wisdom in the Framework of the Old Testament Theology," *Studies in Ancient Israelite Wisdom*, 316.

18. *Les sages d'Israël* (Paris: Du Cerf, 1946); *Le péché originel dans l'Ecriture* (*Lectio Divina* 20 [Paris: Du Cerf, 1958]).

19. L. Alonso Schökel, "Sapiential and Covenant Themes in Gn 2–3," *Studies in Ancient Israelite Wisdom*, 468–80.

20. Cf. J. F. Priest, "Old Testament and the Wisdom Literature," 280, who adds, "Creation faith is by no means limited to the Wisdom tradition."

21. The composer's affinity with nature remains true, whether one takes the poem at face value, or (as does a targum) allegorically, or (in the manner of Gregory Thaumaturgos in the third century) apocalyptically (cf. J. Jarick, "An 'Allegory of Age' as Apocalypse," *Colloquium* 22, no. 2 [1990] 19–27).

22. Cf. the opening verses, *ANET* 596.

23. R. E. Murphy, who rebuts Schmid's wish to see order as the basis of all OT theological statement ("Wisdom and Creation," 9 and n. 19).

24. "Concerning the Structure of Old Testament Wisdom," *Studies in Ancient Israelite Wisdom*, 198.

25. *ANET* 428.

26. Sparks, *The Apocryphal Old Testament*, 681–82.

5

Experience and Observation

We began this work by quoting a character from the Book of Job, Zophar, for his observation that wisdom is many-sided. We quote him more fully in his rebuke of his suffering friend:

> But oh, that God would speak,
>   and open his lips to you,
> and that he would tell you the secrets of wisdom!
>   For wisdom is many-sided (11:5-6).

Job has a lot to learn, says Zophar; as a false sage he is admitting that learning from experience—a source Job appeals to—is inadequate. The book's excellent commentator, Norman Habel, observes: "It is significant that Zophar understands wisdom as having 'secrets,' that is, 'hidden dimensions' which human beings cannot discern with their natural intuition or uninitiated mind."[1]

In fact, all Job's friends want to convince him of their (inadequate) solution for his problems by having recourse to esoteric knowledge—something Job avoids, clinging instead to evidence from his own experience. Echoing Zophar, Elihu also advises Job that "God speaks in one way, and in two, . . . in a dream, in a vision of the night" (33:14-15). Eliphaz also thinks a supernatural intervention will be the kind of thing to bring Job around:

Now a word came stealing to me,
    my ear received the whisper of it.
Amid thoughts from visions of the night,
    when deep sleep falls on mortals,
dread came upon me, and trembling,
    which made all my bones shake.
A spirit glided past my face,
    the hair of my flesh bristled (4:12-15).

Not Visions but Experience

But of course our Job, as the true sage, is unimpressed by this array of heavenly counselors; it is not the stuff of which his skills are made but is better left to charlatans and seers. We discussed above in chapter 2 whether interpretation of dreams is a proper component of Wisdom material and decided that the evidence was against it, a view that book would confirm. Job does not require heavenly revelations to let him puncture the facile generalizations of false sages about suffering and prosperity: the facts are staring them in the face. "The tents of robbers are at peace," he reminds them (12:6), and proceeds at once to invite them to "ask the animals, and they will teach you." No need of visions of the night.

There is no doubt that the epistemology of Wisdom is based on human experience and observation. Biblical and extrabiblical sages are united on that, just as the gnostics will align themselves with Zophar and Eliphaz and Elihu. *Gnosis,* self-acquaintance, is a gift from on high for the elect. The Jesus of *The Gospel According to Thomas* does not instruct his disciples to learn from foxes and fig trees and sparrows but to gain secret knowledge from him: "Jesus said, 'Whoever drinks from my mouth will become like me; I, too, will become that person, and to that person the obscure things will be shown forth.'"[2] *The Apocryphon of John* begins: "The teaching of the saviour and the revelation of the mysteries, which are hidden in silence and which the saviour taught to John."[3]

It is all too spooky for Wisdom, which operates "under the sun," out in the open where anyone with sense and good will can discern truth. "There is an evil that I have seen under the sun, as great an error as if it proceeded from the ruler: folly is set in many high places, and the rich sit in a low place" (Eccl 10:5-6). Qoheleth's beautiful if fatalistic summary of the appropriate times for living and dying, weeping and laughing (3:1-8), was not handed down on tablets of stone or during a vision in the night but dawned upon him after long years of sometimes bitter experience. The authors of Proverbs[4] and Job[5] arrived at similar conclusions from the same process. Ben Sira found that education, travel, peak experiences also contribute to the learning process and that there is no substitute for them:

> An educated person knows many things,
>> and one with much experience knows what he is talking about.
> An inexperienced person knows few things,
>> but he that has traveled acquires much cleverness.
> I have seen many things in my travels,
>> and I understand more than I can express.
> I have often been in danger of death,
>> but have escaped because of these experiences (34:9-13).

Using One's Senses

According to Wisdom's epistemology we are all equipped to acquire wisdom: it is simply a matter of using our senses. Qoheleth quotes an adage on the subject:

> The wise have eyes in their head,
>> but fools walk in darkness (2:14).

A contemporary, author of the Enochic *Book of the Watchers*, stresses repeatedly the advisability of observation of natural phenomena:

> Contemplate all the events in heaven, how the lights in heaven do not change their courses, how each rises and sets in order, each at its proper time, and they do not transgress their law. . . .

> Contemplate how the trees are covered with green leaves, and bear fruit. And understand in respect of everything and perceive how he who lives forever made all these things for you; and how his works are before him in each succeeding year, and all his works serve him and do not change, but as God has decreed, so everything has been done.[6]

The corollary to this epistemological stance is that wisdom is something that can as easily be transmitted as it can be acquired in the first place. Hence Wisdom literature is replete with advice from parents to children and from sages to disciples, whether the setting be family or school, clan or court (as we discussed in ch. 1), and with lectures on the need to listen and observe.

> Hear, my child, and be wise,
> > and direct your mind in the way.
> Listen to your father who begot you,
> > and do not despise your mother when she is old.
> Buy truth, and do not sell it;
> > buy wisdom, instruction, and understanding.
> My child, give me your heart,
> > and let your eyes observe my ways (Prov 23:19, 22-23, 26).

The outcome of all this experience and observation, teaching and learning, was the wise person's equipment for life, a full life, the moral dimension of which we shall examine in the next chapter. It was an equipment that consisted principally not of honors and wealth but of prudence, understanding, shrewdness, insight, discernment—the marks of the true sage. As the Book of Proverbs begins:

> For learning about wisdom and instruction,
> > for understanding words of insight,
> for gaining instruction in wise dealing,
> > righteousness, justice, and equity;
> to teach shrewdness to the simple
> > knowledge and prudence to the young—
> Let the wise also hear and gain in learning,
> > and the discerning acquire skill,

> to understand a proverb and a figure,
>> the words of the wise and their riddles (1:2-6).

Only a fool would neglect such valuable life skills, and so we hear repeatedly that "fools despise wisdom and instruction," "fools hate knowledge" (Prov 1:7; 1:22; 15:32), and so on. These are Wisdom's first principles.

Wisdom and Prophecy

So the skills of authentic sages, biblical and extrabiblical, as distinct from soothsayers and seers, are human skills, acquired and not infused (in the language of the Scholastics) and thus eminently transmissible. They do not properly extend to the realm of the visionary false or true, and the authority they invoke—experience and observation—is different from that of the prophet or lawgiver.[7] Yet for all that, they have God for their source: the sages are always ready to concede that even if it is not constantly on their lips—a case once again of Wisdom's implicit rather than explicit theology, as we noted in the previous chapter. "The Lord gives wisdom," says the author of Proverbs,[8] who speaks frequently of wisdom's source or fountain, as do Ben Sira and *Enoch*.[9] We shall examine more fully in chapter 10 the truly theological framework within which Wisdom operates.

Why, then, do the sages come in for some criticism in Israel's prophetic oracles? Is it because their skills have been acquired independently of the prophetic charism or of the Law given from heaven? Is there some dualistic attitude at work here, a scorn for the merely human, this-worldly attainments of uninspired practitioners? McKane, of course, has reduced the issue to politics, seeing the pragmatic statesmanship of "old wisdom" falling under prophetic attack.[10] At least in places, however, the prophets seem to have in their sights a denatured, exotic profession, not simply the reliance on the human skills of learning and shrewdness we have seen in Israel's sages but employment of visionary techniques by foreigners more typical of apocalyptic than Wisdom. Isaiah of Jerusalem speaks of the limits of their craft that were not being respected by Egypt's sages:

> How can you say to Pharaoh,
>   "I am one of the sages,
>   a descendant of ancient kings"?
> Where now are your sages?
>   Let them tell you and make known
>   what the Lord of hosts has planned against Egypt (19:11-12).

Ezekiel's oracle against the prince of Tyre speaks with derision about a sage playing seer:

> You are indeed wiser than Daniel;
>   no secret is hidden from you.
>
> Therefore thus says the Lord God:
> Because you compare your mind
>   with the mind of God,
> therefore, I will bring strangers against you (28:3, 6-7).

By implication, a sage true to his trade would not be embroiled in such inappropriate techniques.

Wisdom and Law

Likewise, it is not in a spiteful or disparaging way that law-givers and psalmists speak of the limitations of Wisdom by comparison with a divinely given Law. We shall see Sirach and Baruch coming around to the position that the Deuteronomist and psalmist adopt of the relative merits of the two traditions.

> See, just as the Lord my God has charged me, I now teach you statutes and ordinances for you to observe in the land that you are about to enter and occupy. You must observe them diligently, for this will show your wisdom and discernment to the peoples, who, when they hear all these statutes, will say, "Surely this great nation is a wise and discerning people!" (Deut 4:5-6).

> Your commandment makes me wiser than my enemies,
>   for it is always with me.

I have more understanding than all my teachers,
> for your decrees are my meditation.
I understand more than the aged,
> for I keep your precepts (Ps 119:98-100).

There is clearly no lack of esteem by historian or psalmist here for the processes and attainments of Israel's sages; rather, they cite Wisdom in every culture as a benchmark for measuring the superiority of a peculiar gift to Israel in the manner that sage Ben Sira will adopt and transform (if thus restricting) the picture of a universal presence in Proverbs. Jesus, too, will adopt the proverbial material that his generation succeeded to before adding his particular transformation of it. No greater compliment could be paid to people who endeavored by experience and observation—another of Wisdom's faces—to discern the hand of the Lord at work in the world.

Notes

1. *The Book of Job*, 207.
2. Saying 108 (Layton, *The Gnostic Scriptures*, 398).
3. Layton, 28.
4. Cf. 15:16ff.; 16:25; 21:9; 27:14; 28:22-28.
5. Cf. 7:1.
6. *1 Enoch* 3, 5 (Sparks, 186–87).
7. Morgan, *Wisdom in the Old Testament Traditions*, 90–91, doubts that "the real issue between the prophets and the wise was one of authority." Rather, "the basic disagreement seems to center on the ultimate basis of one's loyalty, whether state or nation or Yahweh." He agrees with W. Brueggemann that "in some sense there is an epistemological crisis involved between prophets and the wise" but does not see it as a conflict between reason and revelation; rather, it has to do with the results achieved. Murphy, too ("Wisdom and Creation," 10), would not want a distinction seen between faith and reason—or in other words, as we go on to remark, the sages could not be said to be atheological.
8. Prov 2:6.
9. Cf. *1 Enoch* 48 (Sparks, 229).
10. *Prophets and Wise Men, passim.*

6

The Ways to Life

The fact that serious students of biblical Wisdom could find it adequately summed up as "didactic" and "hagiographic" suggests it obviously has a moral dimension. And although we have argued that such epithets are quite inadequate, that instead Wisdom has many faces, any reader of the Bible's sapiential books will find plenty of instruction on ways to live the good life. Compositions from other cultures and times that can be classed Wisdom material, we have seen, also adopt an instructive role having to do with human behavior. In being didactic, however, some literature from the intertestamental period, by the gnostics, and from Qumran does not always succeed in being authentically sapiential—a reminder once again that the two words are not synonymous.

Ways and Paths

We encounter in Wisdom much advice about the ways to follow in life. Psalm 1 makes no bones about it:

Happy are those
    who do not·follow the advice of the wicked,
or take the paths that sinners tread (v. 1).

Proverbs abounds in this same imagery:

[Wisdom] will save you from the way of evil,
    from those who speak perversely,

> who forsake the paths of uprightness
>> to walk in the ways of darkness,
> those whose paths are crooked,
>> and who are devious in their ways (2:12-13, 15).

There are thus grounds for speaking of the ethical dualism of Wisdom,[1] as of any parenetic material. Parallels with "the way of evil" and "the paths of uprightness" in Proverbs may be found in "the ways of light" and "the ways of darkness" in *The Community Rule* at Qumran and in similar phrases that appear widely throughout ancient Oriental material. *The Testament of Asher* sees it in black and white terms: "Two ways has God appointed for mankind, and two impulses, and two kinds of actions, and two courses, and two ends. Thus, all things are in twos, one over against the other. There are two ways, of good and evil, and along with these are the two impulses in our breasts that make the distinctions between them."[2] Happily, true Wisdom in being *polypoikilos* offers us many other faces to recognize so as to enable us to distinguish it from truly dualistic thinking.

The sages, like moralists in all periods, have no difficulty documenting their teaching on the paths of uprightness and waywardness. As we saw in previous chapters on the human and social dimensions of Wisdom, items stretch from table manners to the requirements of social justice. They include a formidable array of virtues and vices: virtues such as wisdom itself, learning and its synonyms listed in chapter 5, simplicity, loyalty, faithfulness and specifically marital fidelity, honoring the Lord with your substance; vices such as folly itself, hatred of knowledge, greed, complacency, deviousness, crooked speech, stubbornness, scoffing, rejection of advice—the ultimate sin in the estimation of the sages, though they concede the Lord may have a different scale:

> There are six things that the Lord hates,
>> seven that are an abomination to him:
> haughty eyes, a lying tongue,

and hands that shed innocent blood,
a heart that devises wicked plans,
feet that hurry to run to evil,
a lying witness who testifies falsely,
and one that sows discord in a family (Prov 6:16-19).

A Tree of Life

The litany might be thought to be endless and indiscriminate, but there is a kind of consensus that what is involved in wisdom or folly, in cultivating virtues or vices, in following one path or another, is a choice about life or death. At the close of her soliloquy in Proverbs, Wisdom declares that "whoever finds me finds life" (8:35), a sentiment Ben Sira echoes: "Whoever loves her loves life" (4:12). The author of that opening section of Proverbs agrees:

Her ways are ways of pleasantness,
and all her paths are peace.
She is a tree of life to those who lay hold of her;
those who hold her fast are called happy (3:17-18).

Again Ben Sira concurs:

To fear the Lord is the root of wisdom,
and her branches are long life (1:20).

Enoch is aware of the identical choice:

Do not walk in the evil way, or in the way of death! . . .
Walk in the way of peace so that you shall have life.[3]

So amidst all the desultory and pedestrian saws of the sages there could be discerned an elevating and unifying moral vision, that of life and death, a good life and a bad life, expressed in the imagery of trees and fountains and sources of various kinds (reminiscent also of Genesis 2). Until The Wisdom of Solomon there is no eschatological perspective to the vision, it is necessarily and thoroughly this-worldly; but that is not to say it lacks a theology, as we also saw of the sages' implicit cosmology in a previous chapter. Roland Murphy, after myriad studies of Wisdom, appropriately styles a recent attempt *The Tree of Life: An Exploration of Biblical Wisdom Literature.* Some may wish with Von Rad to delay the theologization of Wisdom until "later,"[4] and with McKane to style "old wisdom" pragmatic and unethical.[5] Not only does that settle too readily on the contentious dating of the various bodies of biblical Wisdom, but it also accepts as (moral) theology only what is explicitly theistic and tends to confuse theology with piety. We have tried above to discourage such limited perspectives.

Truisms and Truth

Not that Wisdom in the Bible and beyond always avoids the pragmatic in its morality. We had cause to remark above[6] in examining sapiential attitudes toward women that advice from older men to younger about keeping slave girls and prostitutes (not chastely at arm's length but) in their place reflected pragmatic attitudes on social converse rather than a considered morality—or are the two inseparable?[7] Nor does Wisdom's morality, "late" or "old," always succeed in rising above the shallow and the facile. Job's friends and the prose tale that provides an uneasy framework for the verse disputation articulate the tired truisms that not only fail to rise to the heights of moral vision but have even lost touch with reality. Eliphaz, clutching at the support of purported "visions of the night," rebuts Job's claim to being an innocent sufferer with ineluctable traditional morality:

> Think now, who that was innocent ever perished?
>> Or where were the upright cut off?
> As I have seen, those who plow iniquity
>> and sow trouble reap the same.
> By the breath of God they perish,
>> and by the blast of his anger they are consumed (4:7-9).

Even if the author of the verse dialogue is here holding such morality up to review and critique, pious platitudes can be found in the "old wisdom" of Proverbs and late "legal piety"[8] of the Torah alike:

> Those who despise the word bring destruction on themselves,
>> but those who respect the commandment will be rewarded
>> (Prov 13:13).

Fortunately the unrealism of these moral positions is balanced by the honesty of Wisdom old and late in places in the Bible and beyond. Even before Job, the Sumerian *Man and His God*, Akkadian *Ludlul Bel Nemeqi*, and *The Babylonian Theodicy* had taken a sepia view of life to suggest that an equation of virtue and prosperity in this life does not hold up. Within Israel it could early on be admitted that in real life an ideal value system does not obtain:

> The poor are disliked even by their neighbors,
>> but the rich have many friends (Prov 14:20).

Qoheleth, of course, warms to this theme. Job, despite the lengthy airing of both sides in three cycles of speeches, has no difficulty showing how the alternative position does not square with the facts (e.g., in ch. 21); and a divine judge declares that he, not they, has spoken well of him and discerned true Wisdom in this inequitable universe.

From Wisdom to Apocalyptic

The Wisdom of Solomon, of course, puts all this debate and oscillation into a different context with its long perspective offering "immortality" to the virtuous and discomfiture to their persecutors.

> But the souls of the righteous are in the hand of God,
> and no torment will ever touch them.
> In the eyes of the foolish they seemed to have died,
> and their departure was thought to be a disaster,

and their going from us to be their destruction;
but they are at peace.
For though in the sight of others they were punished,
their hope is full of immortality (3:1-4).

Accordingly, the New Testament can bring together the realism of previous Wisdom with the Hellenistic vision: Jesus does not promise his disciples recompense here and now for their following of him and his value system, *basileia*, but he can offer them the prospect of life hereafter.[9]

But of course Jesus and the author of Wisdom have stepped out of their role as sage when they forecast what awaits the just beyond the grave; both are in an apocalyptic mode, and their discourses take on that flavor. They are not simply reflecting, like Qoheleth and Job, on the inequities of life as experienced but benefiting from an insight that transcends normal human experience. This time we are meant to believe them, unlike Eliphaz with his purported vision of the night. But in all cases the three have parted company with the typical sapiential basis of morality, human experience, which unlike theirs can be verified by tried-and-true criteria. Nothing else is needed to convince Qoheleth that mortals' days are full of pain and their work a vexation. This datum he transforms into his own moral theology by admitting a context that he, like Jesus' disciples and Pseudo-Solomon, recognizes in faith: "There is nothing better for mortals than to eat and drink, and find enjoyment in their toil. This also, I saw, is from the hand of God; for apart from him who can eat or who can have enjoyment?" (2:24-25).

If the sage feels magisterially authoritative, unlike the ruminative Qoheleth, he may not constantly cite the basis for his moral lectures. Ben Sira begins with chapter after chapter of prescriptive maxims (to his school pupils?), not feeling the need to describe life in the raw as the basis for his rules of thumb. His philosophy is obviously that of Von Rad, who opens his *Wisdom in Israel* with the dictum "No one would be able to live even for a single day without incurring appreciable

harm if he could not be guided by wide practical experience"—
and who better than a sage to impart that?

Wisdom and Torah

Ben Sira, however, and some other Jewish literature move
morality one step further from Qoheleth's level of personal experience. They quote the Torah as the basis for the good life in
the belief that it encapsulates more adequately and authorita-
tively both human experience and divine authority, and so it is
beyond question, superior to both sage as empiricist and sage
as teacher.

> How different the one who devotes himself
>   to the study of the law of the Most High!
> He seeks out the wisdom of all the ancients,
>   and is concerned with prophecies;
> he preserves the sayings of the famous
>   and penetrates the subtleties of parables.
> He will show the wisdom of what he has learned,
>   and will glory in the law of the Lord's covenant (39:1-2, 8).

The Torah does not negate human wisdom but confirms and
surpasses it. Whatever wisdom has to recommend it is con-
tained in the Torah, as Ben Sira observes at the conclusion of
the monologue of wisdom personified/hypostatized:

> All this is the book of the covenant of the Most High God,
>   the law that Moses commanded us
>   as an inheritance for the congregations of Jacob (24:23).

Baruch is of the same mind expressed in almost identical
terms, adding the smug benediction that Israel enjoys in the
Torah: "We know what is pleasing to God" (4:4). Qoheleth or
Job could not say as much, though intertestamental composers
will continue the theme.[10]

Has Wisdom thus in a developing Judaism been legalized,
or Law been "sapientialized"? The question engages the scholars.[11] Paul the rabbi, who evidently takes the former view, will

be concerned in 1 Corinthians 1–2 to distinguish wisdom from Torah and from Hellenistic sophistry and to give it a specifically Christian reference in the salvific event that is the death of Jesus,[12] something that on the surface might appear to be folly. But Paul is talking in dogmatic rather than moral terms —about truths rather than behavior—and for him "wisdom" has now taken on a fuller meaning, a reality, a mystery, with many faces, *polypoikilos*. Here we are concerned only with Wisdom's moral face. "Didactic" Wisdom undoubtedly is; yet even this single aspect is susceptible of refinement. Israel at least, in both Testaments, developed its thinking on the ways to life and on the life to which they lead.

Notes

1. As do W. L. Lipscomb and J. A. Sanders, "Wisdom at Qumran," J. G. Gammie and others, eds., *Israelite Wisdom* (Missoula: Scholars Press, 1978) 278.

2. 1 (Sparks, 577–78).

3. *1 Enoch* 94 (Sparks, 296).

4. *Wisdom in Israel,* 298–300 and n. 16.

5. *Prophets and Wise Men,* 47 and *passim.*

6. See page 30.

7. The distinction between manners and morals, Margaret Monro tells us, is one the East does not make (*Enjoying the Wisdom Books* [London: Longmans, 1964] 23).

8. McKane's phrase for the transformed morality of "late wisdom" as a result of prophetic attack (*Prophets and Wise Men,* 109).

9. Cf. Mark 13:9-13.

10. Cf. *1 Enoch* 5; *The Testament of Levi* 13–14.

11. B. S. Childs (*Biblical Theology of the Old and New Testaments,* 189–90) is concerned to resist a simple statement that in the late period Wisdom was absorbed into law, quoting G. T. Sheppard's *Wisdom as a Hermeneutical Construct.* We shall examine Sheppard's position in chs. 10 and 12 below, content for the moment to say that we are happy with his statement of a "wisdom interpretation" (15) of earlier Scripture, while regretting once again that his work is almost entirely confined to a study of Sirach and Baruch.

12. Cf. U. Wilcken on *sophia* in *TWNT:* "Thus Paul, extolling the whole course of election in salvation history, expresses God's plan of salvation in wisdom terms and with wisdom ideas" (7:518).

7
Wisdom's Themes

We have now gone a long way toward answering the question What are the Wisdom composers interested in? They are primarily interested in people, all people: in human nature; in the way people behave, their foibles, their virtues and vices, their skills—thus earning Wisdom the labels "anthropocentric" and "humanistic," as though these were pejorative terms. They are interested in the way people deal with one another honestly and dishonestly, in courtly behavior but not in national and international politics, in the relation of the sexes. They are interested in the real world, in what nature and the animals have to tell us, in the beauties of creation and God's hand in it, in crafts and trades. And in more at this human, social, material level, thanks to their keen observation and distilling of experience, which they weigh up in terms of good and evil.

A Range of Interests

By any standard this is a wide range of interests; the sages' knowledge has rightly been called encyclopedic, with Adam as paradigm and Solomon as their patron.[1] And yet we have seen commentators deprecating their breadth of vision: "The difficulty of the wisdom movement was that its theological base and interest were too narrowly fixed," says one,[2] and another writes of "the omissions in the Wisdom literature."[3] How broad is broad, how narrow is narrow? Can any other body of literature, biblical or extrabiblical, be shown to have such a wide range of interests? The problem, of course, lies with one's understanding of theology and of canon and with how one shapes it to conform to some preconceived model. Objectively, however, one would have to concede that whatever subjects Wisdom does not dwell on, there are an extraordinary number that find a place.

In the following chapters we shall consider Wisdom's stance on a people's historical traditions, whether these are excluded or appear in different guise—Israel's history, for example, the subject of much negative assessment of Wisdom. One can react to biblical Wisdom's stance in various ways. Shock and scandal is one response: "Wisdom has no relation to the history between God and Israel. This is an astonishing fact."[4] Or an attempt can be made to unearth resemblances to key historical themes like covenant, as Luis Alonso Schökel does in the Creation story in Genesis 2–3, where he finds both the hand of a sage and a resemblance to a biblical pattern of covenant-sin-punishment-reconciliation.[5] Or one can refuse to concede the omission of historical themes at all: "Originally therefore [Wisdom] simply took for granted the national dimension of Israel's life and the national functioning of Israel's religion. It did not deny this national dimension, but yet it seldom drew reference to it into the fundamental fabric of its admonitions and insights (although we may cf. Prov 14:28, 34)."[6]

While we shall examine more precisely in the next chapter the place of historical traditions among the traditions biblical Wisdom is interested in, here there is no harm in simply admitting that these are not a dominating sapiential theme in either Old or New Testaments of the Bible any more than they are in the Wisdom material of other cultures. It is worth repeating that the response to this fact depends on one's expectations. It is significant that in the original edition of *Ancient Near Eastern Texts Relating to the Old Testament*, James B. Pritchard collected in section 11 (out of 12) relatively few texts of "Wisdom, Prophecy, and Songs" in comparison to legal and historical texts, whereas in the third edition Wisdom material has loomed large in the addenda. An index of growth in respectability and of changed expectations? We may perhaps speak of a paradigm shift.

Basic Concerns

The sages were too integral in their attitude to life to get carried away with nationalistic concerns, which after all touch people's lives only on the margins. A contemporary example for us is the attention the media give to national and international politics, from which one could gain the impression that that is the stage on which all our lives are lived. The sages knew better: good and evil, living and dying, suffering and thriving—that is where people need the support that comes from experience wisely evaluated and dispensed. So these are the themes that dominate Wisdom in all cultures and periods, from Ptah-hotep in Egypt of the third millennium to *Life's Little Instruction Book,* which concludes with these maxims vital for any youngster:

> Marry only for love.
> Count your blessings.
> Call your mother.

Among the topics, largely moral, that figure in Wisdom are the many we have already listed, skills and deficiencies observable in human beings everywhere, virtues and vices—a lengthy aretalogy, including New Testament Beatitudes and Woes. (Thankfully, consideration of evil in biblical Wisdom does not reach to obsession with its personification in a demonology, as appears in some other literature of the period.)[7] We have also remarked on the balance or imbalance of the reporting; the degree to which certain topics recur, like the adulteress but rarely the adulterer; and the developing assimilation of wisdom as tree of life to a religious code, like the Torah. Beyond these topics and trends in Wisdom material, however, there are certain underlying and continuing concerns or themes that obviously intrigued the sages, just as certain historical and moral concerns intrigued theologians with a historical bent like the Deuteronomist and Chronicler, such as national salvation and restoration. Some themes were of interest to both groups but approached from different standpoints.[8]

An overriding concern for both philosophers and theologians of all types and times is the divine conduct of the universe and its relations with people in particular; we can still read books entitled *The Mind of God.*[9] Wisdom keeps the focus broad to prescind from national boundaries; more nationalistic theologians pose the problem as their god's way of rewarding and punishing their nation and its enemies. Wisdom is engaged in the struggle to discern meaning, pattern—divine Wisdom, in fact—in the confusing and seemingly inequitable economy that is life in the perceivable universe. On the surface, particularly to fools, it does not make sense, and it is unfair—unless one fudges the facts, and only a fool passing for a sage would do that.

Beyond Theodicy

This theme is more comprehensive than theodicy or the riddle of retribution, though it subsumes them. Qoheleth is depressed not only by the injustice of an economy that delivers his hard-won goods to another once he is gone (2:18-21) or because people are unjustly treated by oppressors (4:1-2) but by the fact that the same death awaits human beings and animals alike (3:18-21). He cannot solve the puzzle; he can simply resign himself to the fact that "this also, I saw, is from the hand of God" (2:24)—but a puzzling God nonetheless. It is the larger pattern, not simply justice, that eludes him. No one answers this overarching question for him.

Job, in contrast, is plagued by the injustice of his and others' situation as innocent sufferers.

> Why do the wicked live on,
> > reach old age, and grow mighty in power?
> What is the Almighty, that we should serve him?
> > And what profit do we get if we pray to him? (21:7, 15).

And he believes a day in court would establish that injustice, if not right it. Fortunately for us, we are dealing with a sage who thinks it high time the question is put into context. The response is not personal or social or legal but cosmic in significance. The world reveals to the wise a pattern, a meaning,[10] that defies human wisdom but betrays divine Wisdom, as its author tells Job:

> Who is this that darkens counsel by words without knowledge?
>
> Do you know the ordinances of the heavens?
> > Can you establish their rule on the earth?
>
> Who has put wisdom in the inward parts,
> > or given understanding to the mind?
> Who has wisdom to number the clouds? (38:2, 33, 36-37).

Only with Paul and his vision of the mystery of Christ gathering up all things, things in heaven and things on earth (Eph 1:10)—an *oikonomia* he also styles *sophia*—will such a comprehensive response be given to this search by the sages for meaning. The Wisdom of Egypt and Mesopotamia replicates the questions about retribution that suffering Job poses: *The Admonition of an Egyptian Sage, The Lamentations of Khakheperre -sonbe, A Dispute over Suicide, The Protests of the Eloquent Peasant, A Song of the Harper.* None supplies the definitive answer of the biblical book.

How Does the World Work?

Walter Brueggemann has argued that the Book of Job should be seen as theodicy with a social dimension, lamenting that social systems are not working.[11] He would thus transform the speculative question Why do the innocent suffer into a practical social critique, just as David Freedman[12] transformed it in the case of Second Isaiah to ask, how does history work. I suggest, however, the sage's question—and answer—is even more comprehensive: how does the world work? By divine Wisdom is the reply, not human wisdom. Robert Frost in his *Masque of Reason* has not grasped the full significance of this reply, but at least he neatly states the cutting of the Gordian knot:

> I've had you on my mind a thousand years
> To thank you someday for the way you helped me
> Establish once for all the principle
> There's no connection man can reason out
> Between his just deserts and what he gets.
>
> . . . .
>
> And it came out all right. I have no doubt
> You realize by now the part you played
> To stultify the Deuteronomist
> And change the tenor of religious thought.
>
> . . . .
>
> I had to prosper good and punish evil.
> You changed all that. You set me free to reign.[13]

Brueggemann is conscious of breaking new ground in suggesting Job should be taken as an exercise in criticism of social systems. It is interesting that biblical Wisdom, while lamenting life's inequities, does not proceed to pinpoint such social breakdown in the way Israel's prophets are prepared to, despite a model in Egyptian Wisdom. *The Protests of the Eloquent Peasant*,[14] a lengthy treatise on social justice from the third millennium, depicts the efforts of a poor man to have his rights recognized by a corrupt official. Israel's Wisdom does not warm to the theme beyond generalities.

Creation a Wisdom Theme?

Can we speak of creation as a theme for Wisdom? In chapter 4 we have made a case for a profound and extensive if generally implicit theology of creation in Old Testament Wisdom in comparison with some other sapiential material of the biblical period. The created universe is very much part of the sages' worldview, and they are happy not only to acknowledge it and take it seriously in itself (as distinct from prophetic reference) but also at times to relish its beauties. One thinks of the massive painting of natural marvels in Job that is developed to establish the point of Wisdom present in the world, of Qoheleth's pathetic reminder of the limitations of old age through a series of vivid natural images, of the presence of Wisdom in person at the creation of the world, of the sages' role in creation stories.[15] Nowhere else in the Bible, not even in Jesus' frequent reference to mundane realities for parabolic purposes, is there such extensive acknowledgment of the material universe. Von Rad gives Wisdom credit for the fact that "[Israel] believed man to stand in a quite specific, highly dynamic, existential relationship with his environment."[16]

All this, however, is not to say that the sages were environmentalists, that global survival or abuse of natural resources was on their mind in the way it is a concern and constant theme of today's ecologists. Neither were they pantheists; for Pseudo-Solomon (Wis 13–15) and more prosaic sages idolatry outranks covenant infidelity as capital sin. Theologically they conceded, like Teilhard de Chardin, that the world in which they lived is *le milieu divin,* but they could not have taken the time to compose his *Hymn to Matter*—though they and their New Testament counterpart Paul would supply a sound traditional basis for his doing so. The psalmists, who in their scheme of salvation history in Psalms 135 and 136 included the wonders of creation along with the traditional pattern of the firstborn of Egypt, the Red Sea, Og, and Sihon, had learned from the sages, as have more recent psalmists like Milton, Browning, Blake, Tennyson, Thompson, and Hopkins. Yet to the sages Wisdom in the world was more encompassing than subject for lyrical outburst; Hamlet, concerned for "the whips and scorns of time," is perhaps a more appropriate model.

Notes

1. Cf. Wis 7:17-22.
2. G. E. Wright, *God Who Acts*, 104.
3. R. E. Murphy, *Introduction to the Wisdom Literature of the Old Testament*, 35, 36.
4. "The Place and Limit of the Wisdom in the Framework of the Old Testament Theology," 315.
5. "Sapiential and Covenant Themes in Gn 2–3," 474–75.
6. R. E. Clements, *Wisdom for a Changing World*, 24.
7. Cf. *The Testament of Asher* 1 (Sparks, 578, 581).
8. Donn Morgan discusses the similarities and differences (*Wisdom in the Old Testament Traditions*, 101–2).
9. The title, of course, of a 1992 work by mathematical physicist Paul Davies (New York: Simon & Schuster), taken from the closing words of mathematician Stephen Hawking's *A Brief History of Time*. That today's cosmologists and astrophysicists are engaged in an endeavor not vastly different from the author of Job and Ben Sira is evident from Davies' conclusion: "Through my scientific work I have come to believe more and more strongly that the physical universe is put together with an ingenuity so astonishing that I cannot accept it as brute fact. There must, it seems to me, be a deeper level of explanation. Whether one wishes to call that deeper level 'God' is a mattter of taste and definition" (16). The Bible would probably call Davies' "ingenuity" wisdom.
10. This is a more comprehensive notion than "order" in the universe; Von Rad *(Wisdom in Israel)* and Roland Murphy ("Wisdom and Creation") would surely agree.
11. "Theodicy in a Social Dimension," *JSOT* 33 (1985) 3–25.
12. "'Son of Man, Can These Bones Live?'" *Int* 29 (1975) 185–86.
13. *Selected Poems*, ed. I. Hamilton (Harmondsworth: Penguin, 1973) 233. Murphy, who also notes Frost's interpretation ("Introduction to Wisdom Literature," *NJBC*, 449), like Frost somewhat underestimates the significance of the book's reply: "It is not that Job or Qoheleth provides any 'answers' to the problem of retribution, but they do contribute to living with the mystery of suffering portrayed in the OT."
14. *ANET* 407–10.
15. See my "Dimensions of Salvation History in the Wisdom Books," 105–6.

16. *Wisdom in Israel,* 301. He is closer to the point in recognizing that for the sages "the world has something to say; she actually dispenses truth" (304).

8

Wisdom's Traditions

We can probably judge a society by what it considers important enough to transmit to later generations. Such basic traditions constitute one meaning of "culture," the heritage of a society to which later ages succeed, thanks to the agents of transmission. This culture may not, however, be univocal; what is being passed on as important and even fundamental by one section of society and is therefore able to be classed as a subculture may be largely ignored by another section, which has its own subculture for transmission. In our day, for instance, what is known to an older generation as "fine music" or "the classics" can be disregarded by our youth, who have their own subculture—even if elderly cynics suggest the word is abused in the face of no evidence of cultivation at all.

So the term "tradition" itself is equally ambivalent, as is a word like "custom." For one thing, tradition can mean both the process of transmission and what is transmitted. Likewise, it can apply to the whole of society or just a group within it; it is traditional for me to buy and sell the land I live on, but many of my indigenous compatriots find the idea abhorrent, their traditions about the Land being much less mercenary.

Contexts and Processes

In chapter 1 we canvassed a range of views about the contexts and the traditional processes adopted by the sages in arriving at the Wisdom to which we, if not heirs, at least have access. They included family and clan upbringing, court and scholastic education; the issues involved we need not rehearse again, since it is the other sense of tradition that is of interest here. Of available processes of transmission within a community, cultic recital or reenactment (utilized for celebrating other areas of cultural heritage) was not invoked by the sages,[1] as we shall discuss in the following chapter. Their choice fell rather on oral and written magisterium.

In the previous chapter we raised the question of the themes that predominate in Wisdom material. Here the short answer may again be given to the question Which traditions does biblical Wisdom transmit—namely, very little of historical detail, of the kind that interests composers of Israel's patriarchal history or the Deuteronomist or the Chronicler. Israel's historical traditions are of no great moment to sages of Old or New Testament; Jesus does not constantly bring his audience back to Exodus and Sinai, covenant and conquest, Exile and restoration. It was evidently left to others in the community to perform that traditional role.

Historical Traditions in Wisdom

Sapiential material is therefore the despair of the great tradition historians like Albrecht Alt, Martin Noth, and Gerhard Von Rad. Alt in his influential *Essays on Old Testament History and Religion*[2] of the 1950s and 1960s made no single citation of Wisdom books. Noth was equally dismissive, putting the lacuna down to foreign influence: "On account of its international connections the Old Testament Wisdom was slow to represent any peculiarly Old Testament belief;"[3] and he never mentions Wisdom again in the same volume. Von Rad at first took this view in his *Old Testament Theology*, contemporary with his peers; trying again in *Wisdom in Israel* in 1970, he had to likewise admit "a deep gulf between the intellectual striving of the wise teachers on the one hand and that of the narrators, theologians of history, etc., on the other" (289).[4]

Noth was right to suggest that earlier sapiential material from the Fertile Crescent was no more historically oriented. So, with such encouragement, it has become proverbial to admit of biblical Wisdom, as even Roland Murphy does in 1990, "an absence of any reference to the sacred traditions, such as the patriarchal promises, exodus, Sinai, covenant, etc. The exceptions in Sirach 44–50 and Wisdom 10–19 only prove the rule."[5] In the case of Ben Sira, however, for the sake of precision one should also see him presenting a lengthy if sapientially universalized account of creation and early salvation history at 16:24–17:17 recalling some events from Genesis and Numbers at 16:8-11, reworking sections of the Torah in chapter 29 while omitting any historical details, and giving a rare (for the OT) and again typically sexist reference to the Fall:

> From a woman sin had its beginning,
>   and because of her we all die (25:24).

As Murphy mentions, the conspicuous exceptions to "the omissions in the Wisdom literature"[6] in regard to historical traditions are the two lengthy surveys of salvation history in Sirach and The Wisdom of Solomon. Both demonstrate that these sages (and likewise others?) were not unaware of such traditions or contemptuous of them; a book like Wisdom that can devote over half its length to such a survey (even if this contains a long digression on idolatry arising out of mention of the Egyptians once the Exodus comes into view) cannot be said to lack a sense of history. Of course, it is history with a difference; it is not simply a textual repeat of biblical narrative but a midrashic reworking of the well-known pattern. (We shall see Gerald Sheppard speaking of "a hermeneutical construct for interpreting sacred Scripture.")[7]

History with a Difference

Ben Sira, in a manner akin to Luke's reshaping the genealogy of Jesus to give it a similarly sapiential breadth (Luke

3:23-38), selects an array of Israel's heroes from the beginning—the real beginning, not just with Abraham and patriarchal history but back to Enoch and Noah in humanity's
history. And the basis of choice is not contribution to the "traditional" pattern but their status as figures of wisdom:

> The assembly declares their wisdom,
>> and the congregation proclaims their praise (44:15).

This catholicity and the departure from a "canonical" sequence,
of course, worry those with preconceived notions about biblical traditions; for them "Wisdom has no relation to the history
between God and Israel."[8]

Pseudo-Solomon, too, chooses his litany of heroes on the
same basis, with the same catholicity and the same degree of
respect for "traditional" patterns. It is introduced as the monarch
closes his eulogy of his gift of wisdom as the salvation of hu-
mankind: "And thus the paths of those on earth were set right,
and people were taught what pleases you, and were saved by
wisdom" (9:18). The figures of wisdom—in the history not just
of Israel, predictably—begin with "the first-formed father of
the world" and proceed (with that lengthy digression on idolatry, chs. 13–15) up to the marvels of the Exodus, including
the plagues, in which this apocalyptic "sage" gets carried away,
and has to close his sequence and his book hastily by stating
his theology of history, which pivots on the continuing gift of
wisdom:

> For in everything, O Lord, you have exalted and glorified your
> people,
> and you have not neglected to help them at all times and in all
> places (19:22).

No proper names are supplied, the better to universalize the
message.[9] For him divine Wisdom in the world is manifested
and guaranteed by the gift of wisdom to these heroes.

A Theology of History

There is certainly an awareness of Israel's history in at least these sages; through this awareness they move to a developed theology of human history in sapiential terms. It need not continue to be true, if ever it was, that "so far no one has demonstrated that there was in wisdom a belief in a divine plan for history."[10] The sages, typically, just refuse to be limited to inadequate categories—historical, theological, human. This provides a solution to the conundrum, that while seeming to be not interested in (one pattern of) history, the sages have an (atypical) sense of history.[11] John L. McKenzie in 1967 made the paradoxical remark, "I have identified the wise men of Israel with the historians, and thus effectively designated the historical books as wisdom literature."[12] That is surely to cut the Gordian knot.

Von Rad, trying hard some years later, avoids identifying the two groups and yet views them as responding to a similar challenge by seeing "the late Deuteronomistic history comparable to the later 'theological wisdom' in that it was obliged to present history once again from quite new aspects, that is, that the encounter with history had to be worked through afresh."[13] He is surely right in recognizing in each group a theological approach to history, one group having by far the wider perspective, as we have come to expect of Wisdom. He is less right in implying that such a theology, because implicit, does not inform earlier Wisdom also; the author of Job would subscribe to it, as would Qoheleth with his insistence that all things are in the hand of God, not to mention some of the contributors to Proverbs. As we shall see in chapter 10, the sages' God may not be the God of Abraham, Isaac, and Jacob, but they are nonetheless religious and theological for that.

In any event, it has to be conceded that the traditions of Wisdom are not overtly historical for the most part. We took Jesus as an example of a sage unconcerned to recite the *magnalia Dei* from his own people's story, though his commentators within the New Testament will be anxious that their listeners/readers situate him within the main outline of that story—a dogmatic, not a sapiential, exercise. Other bodies of religious literature from the biblical period are likewise not historical in the way the Jewish story is, making it unique.[14] The Qumran sect has other, more contemporary concerns; the gnostics, while ideologically committed to providing a cosmological myth in place of the biblical Creation account, leave earthly history behind.

Human and Social Traditions

The traditions the sages are mostly engaged in transmitting are human and social traditions—Wisdom's easily recognizable traditional face. That has been true from Ptah-hotep, Ani, and Amen-em-Opet in the Egyptian empire down to Shakespeare's sages and today's *Reader's Digest*. Their advice amounts to living the good life.

> The beginnings of the teaching of life, the testimony for prosperity, all precepts for intercourse with elders, the rules for courtiers, to know how to return an answer to him who said it, and to direct a report to one who has sent him, in order to direct him to the ways of life, to make him prosper upon earth.[15]

> Besides being wise, the Teacher also taught the people knowledge, weighing and studying and arranging many proverbs.[16]

> Son, how can I help you see?
> May I give you my shoulders to stand on?
> Now you see farther than me.[17]

William McKane, we have seen, would want to allow for a distinction between the traditions of the Bible's "old wisdom," which to him amount to "primarily a disciplined empiricism engaged with the problems of government and administration,"[18] and more ethical traditions in "late wisdom." Extrabiblical Wisdom exemplifies both kinds, certainly. What the sages have to say would help their disciples succeed in life without themselves having to undergo the experience or endure the pitfalls. They are universal, catholic, international traditions in generally dealing with human life and human relationships without specific national or political situations in mind. While we can agree with Clements that "it is precisely the absence of this national frame of reference that lends to biblical wisdom its great importance"[19] and add that this feature lends it wider validity, it is also true that much extrabiblical Wisdom tradition is readily transferable, as scholars have noted in comparing Proverbs and Amen-em-Opet. Polonius strides many stages.

Notes

1. Morgan would make an exception for the Psalms: "The evidence of the post-exilic literature, particularly the Psalms, indicates another locus for the major carriers of the wisdom tradition of this period, associated as we have come to expect, with the center of power, the establishment, the cult" (*Wisdom in the Old Testament Traditions*, 135).

2. English trans. (Oxford: Blackwell, 1966).

3. *The Laws in the Pentateuch and Other Essays* (1960), English trans. (Edinburgh and London: Oliver & Boyd, 1960) 89.

4. Donn Morgan, who studies *Wisdom in the Old Testament Traditions*, finds Von Rad's summation misleading: "Even though the wisdom literature itself does not explicitly incorporate nationalistic traditions until Sirach [Von Rad's conclusion, *Wisdom in Israel*, 270], the wisdom tradition, directly and indirectly, was involved and concerned with those traditions which set forth nationalistic and revelatory conceptions of Yahweh" (151).

5. "Introduction to the Wisdom Literature," *NJBC* 447. Cf. B. S. Childs, *Biblical Theology of the Old and New Testaments*, 188: "It is striking to note how little influence one finds from Israel's historical and prophetic traditions on the wisdom corpus."

6. His own phrase, from *Introduction to the Wisdom Literature of the Old Testament*, 35.

7. *Wisdom as a Hermeneutical Construct*, 13.

8. W. Zimmerli, "The Place and Limits of Wisdom," 315.

9. A Catholic translation in 1949—the first since the post-Reformation period—inserts characters' names, the translator Ronald Knox explaining (with no awareness of the theology he was thus resisting), "This chapter [10], in the original, mentions no proper names; a few of them have here been supplied, in accordance with modern usage," and for the next chapter, "The word 'Moses' . . . has been inserted for the sake of clearness" (*The Holy Bible* [London: Burns & Oates, 1954]).

10. J. L. Crenshaw, "Wisdom in the OT," *IDB* 956–57.

11. Roland Murphy wants to assert this ("Wisdom does not view reality in an unhistorical manner": *The Tree of Life*, 113) but is unconvincing in his attempt to show that mention of daily experience by the sages is historical in character.

12. "Reflections on Wisdom," *JBL* 86 (1967) 5.

13. *Wisdom in Israel*, 295.

14. "From Israel's standpoint, this history is not just the ordinary story of wars, population movement, and cultural advance or decline. Rather, the unique dimension of these historical experiences is the disclosure of God's activity in events, the working out of his purpose in the career of Israel. It is this faith that transfigures Israel's history and gives to the Bible its peculiar claim to be sacred scripture." (B. W. Anderson, *The Living World of the Old Testament*, 3rd ed. [London: Longman, 1978] 7–8).

15. Opening of "The Instruction of Amen-em-Opet," *ANET* 421.

16. Eccl 12:9.

17. Opening of *Life's Little Instruction Book*.

18. *Prophets and Wise Men*, 53.

19. *Wisdom for a Changing World*, 23.

9

Wisdom: Sacred or Profane?

Many readers of this book would share the Christian understanding of *faith* as a gift from God, whether one proceeds to see it as a habit or virtue in Scholastic terms or is content with the Old Testament notion of faith as "saying Amen to God" (in Artur Weiser's summary).[1] *Religion*, on the other hand, is man-made: we express our faith relationship with God in forms of our own devising, depending much on our particular culture. This religious expression usually includes elements such as creed, code, cult; through these religious expressions based on their faith people arrive at a meaning system for their lives. At another level believers also wrestle with the implications of their faith, seeking to make sense of what they believe—a *theological* exercise we have seen sages like those represented in Job conducting and (like theologians over the ages) arriving at variously adequate theologies. People at every stage have posed basic theological questions like Job's:

> If I sin, what do I do to you, you watcher of humanity?
>> Why have you made me your target?
>> Why have I become a burden to you? (7:20).

Faith and Religion

While we shall concentrate on the sages as theologians in the next chapter (though, of course, the question has arisen already), it is time to ask the question Does Wisdom have a religious face? Scholars have answered in the affirmative and in the negative. Here again, precision may help. The term "religious" often finds synonyms in "sacred," "sacral," "godly," "other-worldly," and antonyms in "secular," "profane," "ungodly," "this-worldly." We have already had cause to suspect the adequacy of one-word or one-line definitions, especially when these words carry pejorative overtones. A further problem may be that a term like "religious" is thought not applicable to Wisdom at all. "Categories such as 'secular' and 'religious' are quite alien to wisdom and distort the actual development of wisdom which was of a different nature."[2]

To begin at the beginning, can we say all sages are believers, theistic? No. While I am confident we can establish that biblical Wisdom generally has a religious face, a religious dimension, it does not seem to be essential to a sapiential perspective on life and the world that the sage be a believer and express belief in religious terms and forms. "To thine own self be true," Polonius advises his son, invoking no higher authority than human experience. Much of biblical Wisdom strikes one as less replete with references to divine figures than other Oriental material of the kind gathered for us by Pritchard, where there is often a sense of divine nemesis, of which the Bible is healthily free.

> Make offering to thy god, and beware of sins against him. Thou shouldst not inquire about his affairs. Be not too free with him during his procession. Do not approach him too closely to carry him. Thou shouldst not disturb the veil; beware of exposing what it shelters. Let thy eye have regard to the nature of his anger, and prostrate thyself in his name. He shows his power in a million forms.[3]

Tradition historians would be pleased to find this Deuteronomistic vindictiveness in more secularized, less superstitious biblical Wisdom; happily it is absent.

Code and Creed

This is not say, of course, that Qoheleth and the "Words of the Wise" do not betray a deep faith. Fatalist though he too can be, Qoheleth's general conviction about his unspectacular life is that "it is God's gift" (3:13; 5:19); he could hardly be styled ungodly.[4] Although only late in the piece do Israel's sages acknowledge a divinely revealed norm for morality, they can read from human experience and find in it guidance for a proper way of life in accord with the Maker's wishes—a code, in other words. It is experience of life and of the universe that is finally invoked to give evidence of God's true nature in the Book of Job, not the pious but shallow truisms of the prose Job or the friends' preference of heavenly revelations to rigorous analysis of experience. Piety can be as invalid a religious expression of faith as the religious forms criticized by the prophets; one finds, in fact, the repeated acknowledgment of "the fear of the Lord" in the later chapters, 1-9 of Proverbs, somewhat mechanical and unconvincing beside the implicit belief patterns underlying the older material.[5] For Zimmerli (in his more perceptive writing on Wisdom) such underlying patterns constitute the "structure" of Old Testament Wisdom.

> The wise man approaches . . . the entire world with the claim that he comprehends it in the intelligible laws of its operation. Thus, for the wise man, the whole world arranges itself into a scale of values within which every entity has its place, from the immensity of God who is acknowledged as the highest value down to the minute values of good fortune belonging to petty life (joy, satisfaction, happy countenance, etc.).[6]

That should suffice as creed for any religious group, implicit though it be.

Belief also coexists quite comfortably with Wisdom's cosmic dimension, a face turned steadily toward the real world; after all, Israel's belief system hardly encouraged the sages to look to another world. We readily admitted in chapter 4 that they could well be styled this-worldly, secular, in gladly accepting the secularity of a world that is "God's gift," which they above all other biblical composers take seriously and spend time observing—Jesus among them. To be secular, however, is not to be secularist, to deny the existence and role of the divine and live accordingly; that would be the attitude of a fool (Pss 14; 53). Nor should we follow McKane in allowing only late Wisdom to be classed religious, "old Wisdom" having to be castigated as secular. It is a false distinction, different though Qoheleth and Ben Sira clearly are. Precision, we insisted early, is important here, as it is to avoid pejorative connotations of perfectly respectable descriptors like "secular" and "worldly," as Roland Murphy reminds us.[7]

So we should not interpet Wisdom as some primitive death of God theology, anxious like some moderns to disabuse their contemporaries of a three-decker universe and consciously avoid God-talk. They have already achieved the ideals of these latter-day sages in showing how God belongs to the real world of the present at least as legitimately as to the community's past or to an apocalyptic future. Could we say that the sages, like some modern exponents of "secularization theology,"[8] were exponents of a "religionless Judaism," "religionless Yahwism"? Von Rad upbraids H. Gese and H. H. Schmid for thinking Wisdom unaffected by Yahwism[9] and even (tongue in cheek?) suggests late Wisdom is "to be regarded as a form of Yahwism."[10] Certainly Ben Sira is a genuinely pious Jew for whom "the fear of the Lord"[11] is no superficial throwaway but accommodated into his religious mien (cf. 1:11-20; 2:7-17; 34:14-16; 35:22-26), in comparison with the tag some meddler has appended to Job 28.

Wisdom and Cult

But does that still leave the sages apart from and uninterested in cult, worship, liturgy—"religionless" to that extent? Clements sees them supplying for the inadequacies of cult: "Wisdom reminted and reinvigorated the ideas and language of the cultus to suit the needs of scattered communities of Jews living in exile in order to show that 'the fear of Yahweh' still stood as the foundation of all life."[12] Morgan, on the contrary, sees sages and priests being closely related in postexilic Judaism.[13] What do the texts reveal? In general, little cultic reference short of Ben Sira (cf. Eccl 5:1-2, 4-5; Wis 18:9; the prose Job is cultically active) and, considering his orthodox piety, quite a small amount even in him (cf. 7:29-32; 18:22-23; 33:9; 34:21-23; 35:1-13; 38:11; 45:6-22; 50, the priestly Aaron and Simon looming large in the litany of heroes). It is thus perhaps overstating the case to claim that "Sirach introduces us to the sage at worship, singing hymns, and giving voice to prayer."[14]

R. Davidson in *Wisdom in Worship*[15] and particularly L. G. Perdue in *Wisdom and Cult*[16] have studied the matter, the latter chasing all possible references in biblical (and extrabiblical) Wisdom to sacred rituals, sacred psalms, sacred prayer, sacred seasons, sacred places, sacred paraphernalia, sacred personnel, sacred texts. In light of the tenuous textual evidence, his conclusion seems suitably general: "The traditional wise regarded the realm of cult to be an important compartment within the orders of reality, and therefore merited sapiential scrutiny and demanded sagacious participation."[17] Perdue would thus be contesting Von Rad's admission of "the gulf between the wise men and things cultic."[18]

It seems that once again the question of Wisdom's religious face is bedeviled by lack of precision, as it also bedevils modern discussion of the secular and the religious. To admit that Jesus and the Old Testament sages are not found constantly at worship does not call faith into question. Is it a matter for regret that we are asked to pray to "our father in heaven" rather than the God of the patriarchs? Are we disappointed that biblical Wisdom cannot parallel the pantheon of extrabiblical Ahiqar? If the sages are less interested in cult than the Chronicler (and, with due respect to Perdue, we have to admit it), that does not diminish the creed to which they subscribe from the beginning, implicit though this may generally be, and the code they constantly impart, little though they may acknowledge Sinai tablets as its basis. Would sacralization of either have promoted the sages' service of their contemporaries? Today's secularization theologians would not agree.

Wisdom's Religious Integrity

The integrity of Wisdom is one of its great virtues, as it is also a potent message to us in our day. Life is not divisible into sacred and profane. God is active in all creation and among all people; not only liturgical misdemeanor but any social or moral abuse constitutes an "abomination,"[19] as Proverbs reminds us. The earliest sages are religious in this sense[20] if not all as pious or cultic as Ben Sira. So we need not be either defensive or condemnatory of them—just sufficiently nuanced in our thinking about their faith, their religion, and their role as theologians. Claus Westermann could recall this before saying of them that their purpose "requires neither revelation nor theological reflection. Wisdom is secular or profane."[21] It is bad enough to misread the sages; to suggest that their interest (and Paul's) in God's entire creation renders them irreligious is a myopia we have outgrown—thanks to them.

Notes

1. *pisteuo, TWNT* 6, English trans. (Grand Rapids: Eerdmans, 1969) 186.

2. B. S. Childs, *Biblical Theology of the Old and New Testaments,* 188–89. Roland Murphy seems to want to have it at least two ways: "Many have sought to distinguish between 'profane' and 'sacred' within the body of the sayings. Such a procedure can hardly escape an anachronistic judgement; our criteria for distinguishing the two differ from those of ancient Israel. That is why we have preferred to distinguish merely between experiential wisdom (e.g., Prov 10ff.) and the more explicitly didactic or formative wisdom (e.g., Prov 1–9). But for the sages

all of this had a sacred or religious bearing—even conduct at the table" (*Introduction to the Wisdom Literature of the Old Testament*, 32).

3. "The Instruction of Ani," *ANET* 420.

4. Cf. also 2:24-25; 5:18, 20; 8:15.

5. J. B. Crenshaw holds for a "deep religious cast of wisdom from its earliest stages" ("Method in Determining Wisdom Influence upon 'Historical' Literature," 483).

6. "Concerning the Structure of Old Testament Wisdom," 198.

7. *The Tree of Life*, 113.

8. For a summary of the modern movement and its slogans, see R. L. Richard, *Secularization Theology* (New York: Herder & Herder, 1967).

9. *Wisdom in Israel*, 10.

10. Ibid., 307.

11. This is an attitude of OT Wisdom that for Roland Murphy is characteristic. Cf. his article "Religious Dimensions of Israelite Wisdom," *Ancient Israelite Religion: Essays in Honor of Frank Moore Cross*, ed. P. D. Miller, P. D. Hanson, and S. D. McBride (Philadelphia: Fortress, 1987) 449–58. "Although wisdom seems to be taken up with the ordinary, everyday events, it retains its basic relationship to God, and the fear of the Lord is an essential ingredient in this achievement" (456).

12. *Wisdom for a Changing World*, 35; cf. 29: "Instead of holiness the concept of 'the fear of the Lord' becomes for the teachers of wisdom the primary concept which is held to be the motivating impulse for all right acting and right thinking. Undoubtedly this phrase, like the language of holiness, was originally cultic in its origin."

13. "With the establishment of a hierarchical cultic power structure in post-exilic Israel, it is generally assumed that the scribes are much more closely attached to the cult—indeed, most of them are priests" (*Wisdom in the Old Testament Traditions*, 120).

14. Crenshaw, "Wisdom in the OT," *IDB* 955.

15. (London: SCM, 1990).

16. Society of Biblical Literature Dissertation Series (Missoula: Scholars Press, 1977).

17. Ibid., 362.

18. *Wisdom in Israel*, 187.

19. Clements, *Wisdom for a Changing World*, 33: "The concept of 'abomination' has migrated far from its original cultic, and taboo-laden, setting. It is synonymous with 'socially and morally reprehensible conduct.'"

20. Cf. J. F. Priest: "There is no evidence that Israelite wisdom ever was secular" ("Where Is Wisdom to Be Placed?" 283–84). Wisdom was always implicitly religious, he says; and even in Sirach there is a mixture of secular and religious material.

21. *Elements of Old Testament Theology* (Atlanta: Knox, 1982) 100.

10

The Theology of Wisdom

There are strangely contradictory opinions about the theological character of Wisdom for the same reason we found such divergence in views about its religious face, namely, imprecision in the use of terms. In the eleventh century St. Anselm of Canterbury in his work on theology, *Proslogion*, happily supplied us with a classic definition in entitling it *Fides quaerens intellectum*, faith in search of understanding. He took up the ticklish question of the relationship between faith and reason investigated six centuries earlier by his illustrious predecessor, Augustine of Hippo, in many places but particularly in his Sermon 43 on Isaiah 7:9 (in the Septuagint reading). The great African, with typical paradox, had coined the formula for this relationship, *Intellege ut credas, crede ut intellegas:* Understand with a view to faith, have faith with a view to understanding.[1] Encouraged by this (to both great theologians) bold elevation of human reason, Anselm explains the theological endeavor to his readers: "I have written this little work from the viewpoint of persons trying to raise their mind to contemplate God and seeking to understand what they believe."[2]

Faith Seeking Understanding

The authors of the Sumerian *Man and His God*, the Akkadian *Ludlul Bel Nemeqi, The Babylonian Theodicy*, Qoheleth,

Job, and their myriad successors to our time have set about this task, especially but not solely when confronted with life's troubles, asking, "Why me?" Faith will take us only so far; the human spirit asks also for understanding. We need a world-view in which we can make sense of what we believe. A great merit of the sages is that they achieved this.

Why, then, the reluctance to see theology in Wisdom? Perhaps, unlike Augustine and Anselm, we are prepared to settle for an etymological definition of theology as a study of God. Unless God is constantly and explicitly in focus—and a God of our choosing—it is not vintage theology. We saw Claus Westermann declaring Wisdom to have an interest in "neither revelation nor theological reflection."[3] Only a God who comes to us through formal epiphany can convert our rumination to theologizing; Pseudo-Solomon[4] and Paul in his wake[5] will reject this view, of course. Others, however, have been equally dismissive: "For wisdom, questions of faith entered in only on the periphery of its field. It works with reason, in its simplest form as sound common sense. . . .What this wisdom teaching has to say only passes over into theology where the subject-matter contains some kind of pointer or reference to Jahweh, his activity, or what pleases or displeases him."[6] So much for Augustine and Anselm.

There is, of course, no dichotomy between faith and common sense—though the relationship needs exploring, as those patristic figures did and as the biblical sages provided living exemplar. (We conceded above that not every wise person is necessarily a believer.) Augustine in that sermon, in fact, aware that some may be scandalized by his speaking of human understanding in the same breath as divine faith, justifies the role played by his own commentary on the sacred text: "I will explain in a nutshell how to take this without arousing controversy: Understand my word with a view to faith, have faith in God's word with a view to understanding." That is precisely the role the biblical sages discharged for their disciples: in the light of faith they read and explained God's design from the pages not of a sacred text like Augustine at that point but of the world around them. As even Von Rad admits of them, "The world has something to say [to them]; she actually dispenses truth,"[7] and this truth they could dispense to others. Faith *and* common sense made this ministry a theological exercise.

The psalmists who reshape the pattern of salvation history to include creation of the sun and the moon and the stars (Pss 93; 104; 135; 136), Qoheleth depicting the onset of old age in natural images and "the breath returning to God who gave it" (12:7), Job accepting the evidence of divine transcendence in the world around him—how does this not qualify as true theology?[8]

> If one wishes to contend with him,
> > one could not answer him once in a thousand.
> He is wise in heart, and mighty in strength
> > —who has resisted him, and succeeded?—
> he who removes mountains, and they do not know it,
> > when he overturns them in his anger;
> who shakes the earth out of its place,
> > and its pillars tremble;
> who commands the sun, and it does not rise;
> > who seals up the stars;
> who does great things beyond understanding,
> > and marvelous things without number (Job 9:3-7, 10).

Theology's Proper God

A problem about acknowledging the truly theological character of Wisdom from (prebiblical and) early Proverbs onward has been that biblical theology has been the preserve of the historians, for whom the God of the patriarchs and Sinai has alone been acceptable. This is generally not Wisdom's God prior to Baruch and Sirach; rather, it is a kindly if mysterious Providence who moves through the pages of Wisdom literature, a God who is interested in all peoples and has not confined divine activity within the history of Israel. How could this literature qualify as theology if "the concepts of cult, saving history, and people of God apparently lie outside [its] field of vision"?[9]

Fortunately, even in the heyday of the tradition historians there was the odd lone voice lamenting (as Toombs did in 1955) that "as long as Old Testament theology is represented exclusively in terms of the history, institutions and cultus of the Hebrew people, it will exclude the wisdom literature by definition."[10] In the intervening four decades, with a decline in exclusive attention to historical material in the Bible in favor of the sapiential, we have had the opportunity to see the God of legitimate theology more comprehensively and recognize the validity of the sages' God. "In Israel we should view the attitude of the wise, not as non-theological over against a religious tradition dominated by a view of God who revealed himself in historical events, but rather as an alternative and equally valid way of doing theology."[11] Well and good; this greater breadth allows us to also think of Jesus, Egyptian and Mesopotamian sages, and other Wisdom figures when we consider the extent of Wisdom's theological face. "Our father in heaven" should be an acceptable reference point when we theologize.[12]

A Late Theology?

So it is high time to take issue with an attitude to Wisdom theology not yet dead, namely, the tendency to concede a theological character only to later compositions because of the explicit theologizing of pious sages like Ben Sira. It is the canon-within-the-canon syndrome all over again; Von Rad speaks of "a 'theologization' of wisdom" when dealing with Proverbs 1–9, Job, and Sirach[13] in comparison with earlier Wisdom. Others have likewise spoken of a graduated "process of theologizing" in chronological terms.[14] Gerald Sheppard in *Wisdom as a Hermeneutical Construct: A Study in the Sapientializing of the Old Testament* concentrates exclusively on Sirach and Baruch in arriving at his understanding of a "wisdom interpretation" by the late Old Testament of earlier compositions;[15] in chapter 8 we saw this occurring particularly in Sirach.

While there is validity in both these viewpoints, chronological and hermeneutical, their effect is to downplay the full theological value of Wisdom. Even in the later works the sages' theological activity is not confined to review of past compositions, Torah and Prophets, though we have shown that these stand to benefit from a sapiential universalizing. For instance, Ben Sira looks around the world of his time and evaluates it in the light of his theology, for example, upholding the worth of mundane trades and professions (see p. 41 above). If we concede that the theology of the personification/hypostatization of wisdom in Proverbs 8, Sirach 24, and Wisdom 7 and the assimilation of wisdom to Torah in Sirach and Baruch is a rarefied insight in comparison with the more mundane, secularized observation of proverb makers and dyspeptic commentators in Proverbs and Ecclesiastes, are we not in danger once again of reserving theology to more religious material and confusing theology with piety? And are we not failing to recognize both implicit and explicit theologizing by the sages, as we found to be true of commentators on Wisdom's creation theology in chapter 4?

Theology's Big Questions

Because, in fact Wisdom—all Wisdom, early and late, biblical and extrabiblical—does broach the big theological issues, if sometimes more moral than dogmatic. Being less nationalistic allows it to do this, we have seen. Theodicy, soteriology, cosmology—they are all there. What does it mean to live in this inequitable world? How does one square human and divine commitments? What rewards and punishments, divine and human, operate in the observable economy? How does one cope with life's injustices? How did we get into this mess? To where can we look for relief, redemption, salvation? Is death the end of everything? Is there pattern, meaning in it all?

The gods who lived formerly rest in their pyramids,
The beatified dead also, buried in their pyramids.
And they who built houses—their places are not.
See what has been made of them!

. . . .

Make holiday, and weary not therein!
Behold, it is not given to a man to take his property with him.
Behold, there is not one who departs who comes back again![16]

My companion says not a true word to me,
My friend gives the lie to my righteous word.
The man of deceit has conspired against me,
And you, my god, do not thwart him.[17]

Do not fret because of the wicked;
   do not be envious of wrongdoers,
for they will soon fade like the grass
   and wither like the green herb.
Trust in the Lord, and do good;
   so you will live in the land, and enjoy security.[18]

Surely I am too stupid to be human;
   I do not have human understanding.
I have not learned wisdom,
   nor have I knowledge of the holy ones.
Who has ascended to heaven and come down?
   Who has gathered the wind in the hollow of the hand?[19]

Sages from earliest times have pondered the question of *retribution,* even if only with Pseudo-Solomon's more apocalyptic vision is an eternal perspective finally provided to drastically alter the pattern. From Egyptian "Instructions" through *Ahiqar* and *1 Enoch* to Paul goes the search for order in the universe. The Genesis text can be read to suggest that "an author familiar with the sapiential milieu asks himself: Where does *evil* come from? He answers: from *sin.* And where does everybody's sin come from?"[20] Ben Sira will put the blame squarely on woman, in accord with that story (25:24). And from where will rescue come? For Wisdom *"salvation* is not brought about by Yahweh descending into history nor by any kind of human agency such as Moses or David or one of the patriarchs, but by specific factors inherent in the creation itself."[21] No, the sages do not dodge the big theological issues, varying though the adequacy of their insights prove to be.[22]

Sages, Deuteronomist, Yahwist

Wisdom, in fact, could be compared with the more "respectable" biblical theologians in their approach to such theological issues—and compared favorably. Von Rad admits a comparability of (late) Wisdom with the Deuteronomistic school as an attempt to face major issues for Israel;[23] even formally there are resemblances, says Morgan, as in the use of the parenetic style that is torah.[24] We have quoted with approval poet Robert Frost (p. 70 above) to the effect that in the Book of Job the sages broke through the Deuteronomistic shackles imposed on the question of retribution, for which, however, earlier "traditional" Wisdom has to shoulder some of the blame; the question was susceptible of a more profound response than Proverbs or Job's friends were bent on offering.

The favorable light shed on Wisdom in comparison with other biblical theologies derives principally from its wide perspective, its universalism. Even if resemblances can be found to Yahwistic[25] and Deuteronomistic approaches, Wisdom gains from—as in the past it has suffered from—its unwillingness to be confined in a narrow historical, nationalistic vision. All of the observable world falls under its theological—because faith-filled and common-sense—scrutiny; the condition of all people and things are found relevant by the sages, and attempts are made to read the face of God—the God of all people and things. *Nihil humanum alienum,* says the poet, to which Wisdom would add *nec creatum nec divinum.* If late Wisdom is given credit for being more theological, in a sense it should be faulted for reducing the dimensions of this theological scrutiny, if admittedly raising the tone. Yes, Wisdom indisputably has a theological face—and a contemporary face at that. Augustinian and Anselmian, too, thank goodness.

Notes

1. *CCL* 41, 512.

2. *Proslogion*, proem., ed. M. J. Charlesworth (Oxford: Clarendon, 1965) 102.

3. *Elements of Old Testament Theology*, 100. Westermann, of course, is also author of *The Promises to the Fathers*, English trans. (Philadelphia: Fortress, 1980).

4. Wis 13:1-9.

5. Rom 1:18-21.

6. G. Von Rad, *Old Testament Theology* 1, 435, 437.

7. *Wisdom in Israel*, 304.

8. Cf. my "Dimensions of Salvation History in the Wisdom Books," and ch. 3 of *Jesus and the Mystery of Christ*.

9. Von Rad, *Old Testament Theology* 1, 452.

10. "Old Testament Theology and the Wisdom Literature," *JBR* 23 (1955) 195.

11. R. Davidson, *Wisdom and Worship*, 14.

12. We recall Paul endeavoring to theologize with the Areopagus in Athens in terms of "the God who made the world and everything in it" (Acts 17:24), whereas with the Jews in the synagogue in Pisidian Antioch (Acts 13) he could make meaningful reference to the God of their fathers.

13. *Wisdom in Israel*, 300, n. 16. McKane, of course, made his division of "old" and "late" Wisdom partly in these terms, too. Morgan contests the division allowed by Von Rad, McKane, and Michael V. Fox, "Aspects of the Religion of the Book of Proverbs," *HUCA* 39 (1968) 55–70 (*Wisdom in the Old Testament Traditions*, 60).

14. Crenshaw, "Wisdom in the OT," 955, distinguishing three stages; Morgan, *Wisdom*, 145, concurs. Murphy, *Introduction to the Wisdom Literature of the Old Testament*, 44–45, sees it as a result of Wisdom departing from the court for the school in the postexilic period.

15. "At a certain period in the development of Old Testament literature, wisdom became a theological category associated with an understanding of canon which formed a perspective from which to

interpret Torah and prophetic traditions. In this sense wisdom became a hermeneutical construct for interpreting sacred scripture" (13).

16. "A Song of the Harper," *ANET* 467.

17. "Man and His God," *ANET* 590.

18. Ps 37:1-3.

19. Prov 30:2-4.

20. L. Alonso Schökel, "Sapiential and Covenant Themes in Gn 2–3," 479 (emphasis added).

21. Von Rad, *Wisdom in Israel*, 314 (emphasis added).

22. Feminists, of course, find only some aspects of Wisdom theologically attractive.

23. He sees "the late Deuteronomistic History comparable to the later 'theological wisdom' in that it was obliged to present history once again from quite new aspects, that is, that the encounter with history had to be worked through afresh" (*Wisdom in Israel*, 295).

For Zimmerli, on the contrary, there is no comparison: "If we compare the historical work of the Deuteronomistic writer or the words of the prophets, we can see very clearly the difference between them and the words of the wise man" ("The Place and Limit of the Wisdom in the Framework of the Old Testament Theology," 315).

24. *Wisdom in the Old Testament Traditions*, 101.

25. "From the outset, intentionally or not, the wisdom tradition is tied closely to the major Yahwistic interpretation of Israel's history" (Morgan, *Wisdom*, 139–40). Von Rad also sees that theological Wisdom "is to be regarded as a form of Yahwism" (*Wisdom in Israel*, 307).

11

The Formal Face of Wisdom

We are nearing the end of our study of Wisdom and have continued to make the point that discerning the overall sapiential perspective is more demanding than simply settling for one or another aspect or dimension or "face." That is true likewise of the search for human wisdom; it cannot be acquired as easily as mere knowledge of facts, as the sages would be the first to insist. It is a temptation in the acquisition of any art to fix upon one external, easily recognizable feature and convince oneself that the essence has now been attained. So many graphic "artists" fall short of true art because of finding a facility in forms alone; "poets" can fail here, too. Skills, like any habit, can be acquired by dint of repetition; soul, insight, vision is something rarer and may never be acquired, no matter how much one is formally proficient.

Vision and Form

This distinction is important for neophytes to understand in approaching any literary study. How often will young students speak of "poetry" when all they have recognized is the verse form in which the vision (which may not be poetic at all) is expressed. The corollary is that true poetic vision can take a prose form—and be dismissed for doing so; yet Ruskin can be as poetic as Wordsworth. One therefore comes to distrust form as a reliable index or characteristic of particular literary divisions where different insights or ways of approaching reality, or world-views, may take the same form—or, vice versa, one vision may take a variety of forms.

Wisdom is particularly fraught with this confusion. We have noted the readiness of some commentators to begin their discussion of the topic with attention to forms, even perhaps while lamenting the effect this has on readers of Wisdom literature.[1] The effect, in fact, is that Old Testament Wisdom is immediately associated in many people's minds with the proverb, and anything more periodic in style is thought less typically sapiential, like the verse dialogue in Job, Qoheleth's meandering, the Hellenistic periods of Wisdom of Solomon, not to mention extrabiblical material aside from the proverbs of Amen-em-Opet. Likewise, Jesus as a sage is identified with the parable, much less with the proverb. We can be surprised to learn that Jewish sages before him employed that parabolic form, as we likewise encounter less comment on his overall sapiential outlook.[2] In other words, attention to forms in literature both ancient and modern can obscure the vision that lies behind them and that provides them with their true characteristics.

A Range of "Wisdom Forms"

So Wisdom has a formal face—in fact, a face that could almost be described as *polypoikilos* in itself. We have deliberately left it till last to suggest its distance from the heart of Wisdom—and perhaps to offset the prominence forms are sometimes given. Today, as we mentioned in chapter 1 about the pansapiential current in biblical study, a whole range of forms are being classified Wisdom forms insofar as scholars trace Wisdom influences in other material or isolate forms beyond the proverb and parable found in acknowledged Wisdom. To compile a list of them—sages are given to listing, remember—is presumptuous, as the number is constantly growing; but you will find the following included by one scholar or another in "Wisdom forms":

proverb	law, prohibition
riddle	exhortation
fable	torah
parable	woe oracle
numerical formula	psalm
allegory	prayer
dialogue, disputation	beatitude/macarism
autobiographical narrative	onomasticon/list
didactic narrative	historical retrospect
didactic/rhetorical question	apocalyptic.[3]
hymn	

Such forms can also be documented and in fact augmented from extrabiblical material: Egyptian Instructions and proverbs, Pharaoh Amen-em-het I's autobiographical narrative in his Twelfth Dynasty Instruction, the exhortation and prohibitions of Ani, the lamentations of Khakhaperre-sonbe, a man's dialogue with his soul in *A Dispute over Suicide,* the Akkadian fable *Dispute Between the Date Palm and the Tamarisk,* Qumran hymns and beatitudes, *The Sayings of Ahiqar, The Psalms of Solomon,* and so on.

Where to Now?

Sight of this growing list of forms that are declared "Wisdom" forms, either because they are characteristic of Wisdom or can be documented from it, prompts some initial responses. What is left that is not a Wisdom form, especially if torah, apocalyptic, and woe oracle can be classed as Wisdom forms? Many of the above can be documented also from Torah and Former and Latter Prophets, not to mention apocalyptic, Psalms, and other poetry/verse within the Bible. Does all literature that includes such forms become ipso facto sapiential? Does the occurrence of such forms, say in prophet or historian, provide a clue of Wisdom influence? Amos, for instance, has been found by Samuel Terrien and H. W. Wolff to have undergone such influence by reason of the occurrence of forms like numerical formulae, exhortation speeches, didactic/rhetorical questions, and woe oracles.[4] This is even independent of the occurrence of "Wisdom vocabulary"; Crenshaw tells us that "wisdom shares a common vocabulary with prophecy, priestly discourses, and historiography"[5]—and why not psalms? Then there are "Wisdom themes and concerns," likewise found elsewhere. How can we ever arrive at anything specifically sapiential—or specifically torah or prophetic, for that matter?

One general conclusion is that literary styles in ancient literature are (or should be) becoming less identified with particular literary/theological perspectives. Sages and theologico-historians can be equally moralistic, even if their theological roots, reference points, and conclusions can be diverse; so it is not surprising if both have recourse to torah and parenesis at times. Readers of Proverbs 6:20-35 could be pardoned for thinking they had strayed into Deuteronomy.

Form an Unreliable Index

The corollary is that form is the least reliable index of Wisdom material. We may encounter proverbs in history (cf. 1 Sam 24:13; 1 Kgs 20:11) and prophecy (Jer 13:23), fables in Torah (cf. Num 22:21-35) and Prophets (cf. Ezek 17:1-10), numerical formulae in Hosea (6:2) and Amos (1:3-6), parables in Isaiah (5:1-3) and 2 Samuel (12:1-4), hymns and psalms and exhortations all over the Old (and New) Testament. That does not guarantee that in any such example we have struck a lode of genuine sapiential material; one swallow doesn't make a summer (if one may become parabolic for the moment).

Which leads us into a final chapter and its conclusion, that there is an easily recognizable and definitively reliable perspective in Wisdom that preserves us from the need for a superficial and questionable recourse to formal features. Correlatively, other bodies of biblical and extrabiblical literature can also be identified not for formal features but for the perspective they adopt in viewing reality. Von Rad could be forgiven for believing that Wisdom rather than prophecy proved a more likely basis for the development of apocalyptic, considering the universal attitude adopted by the sages, in contrast with the parochialism of Israel's prophetic traditions. But the two bodies of material nonetheless are easily distinguishable by their tone, climate, and degree of contact with the real world, no matter which forms their authors choose to employ for their message. The author of James could never have composed the Book of Revelation.

Notes

1. Roland Murphy we mentioned in this regard in ch. 1. Naturally, in one study of his, *Wisdom Literature*, The Forms of Old Testament Literature 13 (Grand Rapids: Eerdmans, 1983), he is committed to a concentration on formal aspects while regretting that the term "wisdom literature" is misleading in directing attention solely to literary remains (3). It is ironic that a reviewer of his *Tree of Life* could remark: "One limitation of Murphy's work is that little attention is paid to the form of wisdom literature" (David Bland, *Int* 46, no. 2 [1992] 184).

2. It is not simply a matter of distinguishing practical from speculative Wisdom, as though peeling husk from kernel, as William Beardslee is inclined to suggest in directing attention to Jesus' use of the proverb in the wake of earlier study of the other manifestation of Jesus' practical Wisdom, the parable ("Uses of the Proverb in the Synoptic Gospels," *Int* 24 [1970] 61–73). Jesus' sapiential outlook appears as much in proverb and parable as it does in utterances as wisdom hypostatized, even if the tone is different (as we discussed in regard to Wisdom's theological face in the previous chapter); perhaps we can speak instead of a "high" and "low" Wisdom theology.

3. For the meaning of these categories, see J. Crenshaw, *Old Testament Wisdom: An Introduction*, 36–39, "Wisdom in the OT," *IDB* 953–54.

4. Cf. D. Morgan, *Wisdom in the Old Testament Traditions*, 66–70. Morgan also talks of styles and forms that Wisdom has in common with the Deuteronomist (96–98).

5. "Wisdom in the OT," 953.

12

Conclusion:
The Perspective of Wisdom

This book began, not always affirmatively, with some references to Job. Zophar gave us a title in assuring us that Wisdom is "many-sided," but we had to admit he is a discredited character, his credentials as a sage being tarnished by his dependence on ESP. Job—if he is the speaker in that likewise suspect chapter 28, an "erratic intrusion" into the dialogue[1]—embarked on a search for the location of wisdom, but finally ended up with an insight into the very nature of Wisdom. The book has continued to puzzle interpreters; Job's insight has not dawned on all. Donn Morgan tells us we know less rather than more about Wisdom. "At the present time there are several different notions about the historical and theological development of wisdom, no one definition of wisdom capable of winning consensus, much disagreement about the social setting and class of wisdom, and a lack of unanimity about the nature and development of some fundamental literary forms."[2] Well might the Job of chapter 28 ask, "Where shall wisdom be found?"

Can we presume the sages themselves knew, even if they were not good at keeping to the point on the matter but strayed off, like Job, onto the question of location? Ben Sira made a confident start, though likewise thinking first of origin and location:

All wisdom is from the Lord,
　　and with him it remains forever.
The sand of the sea, the drops of rain,
　　and the days of eternity—who can count them?
The height of heaven, the breadth of the earth,
　　the abyss, and wisdom—who can search them out?
Wisdom was created before all other things,
　　and prudent understanding from eternity.
The root of wisdom—to whom has it been revealed?
　　Her subtleties—who knows them?
There is but one who is wise, greatly to be feared,
　　seated upon his throne—the Lord.
It is he who created her;
　　he saw her and took her measure;
　　he poured her out upon all his works,
upon all the living according to his gift;
　　he lavished her upon those who love him (1:1-6).

Wisdom Beyond wisdom

Like the Job of chapter 28 and the book's author, Ben Sira got beyond the quality of being wise to a divine Wisdom that can be observed in all God's works, as Pseudo-Solomon and Jesus and Paul would so observe it. Like a Scholastic theologian and not unlike the Akkadian author of *Ludlul Bel Nemeqi* praising Marduk, lord of wisdom, he could see it as a divine perfection in which created nature can share. Unlike the gnostic *sophia* it is superior to mere *gnosis* and eminently desirable. In endeavoring to arrive at the meaning of Wisdom, both biblical and extrabiblical authors realize their goal lies beyond the quality of being wise; sapiential literature has a wider focus. As the author of a modern allegory *The Alchemist* says through his title character, "The wise men understood that this natural world is an image and a copy of paradise. The existence of this world is simply a guarantee that there exists a world that is perfect. God created the world so that, through its visible objects, men could understand his spiritual teachings and the marvels of his wisdom."[3]

So we too have been concerned in these pages with Wisdom literature and the many faces of Wisdom. Though concentrating on biblical and particularly Old Testament sages, we have tried to contextualize these by also glancing at other compositions of the biblical period and before it, so as to gain the better appreciation that can come from comparison. We might well have looked at more Wisdom material from our own time, not prepared to concede with Von Rad that there is nothing in our day comparable with ancient Wisdom.[4] The questions faced by Proverbs, Qoheleth, and the author of Job are timeless and universal, as much older works from other cultures have confirmed; the study of human nature and behavior and social converse as well as natural creation continues to occupy people, different though the forms may now be that such musings take and the contexts in which our contemporary sages operate in McLuhan's "electric age"—newspapers, churches, schools, the occult, psychoanalysis, talk radio, movies, television.

Wisdom's Many Faces

Our thesis has been twofold: that Wisdom has many faces, and that these many faces constitute a distinctive Wisdom perspective on reality and the questions arising. The former conviction we took from Zophar and from Paul: Wisdom is *polypoikilos,* multicolored, many-faceted, many-sided, multidimensional, of a rich variety. The sapiential is no simple, monochrome view of reality. There is a human, or anthropological, side to Wisdom—the way it looks at people, being interested in human nature and behavior, seeing people in universal categories of good and evil rather than racial or national groups. It has a social face, concerned with relationships, not least the way women and men are placed in society. It has a cosmic, material, this-worldly aspect, spending time studying the real world, animals and nature included. Wisdom has an epistemological face, you might say, gaining its insights not from intuition or revelation but from experience and observation. It has a moral face, a distinctive thematic and traditional face, and, equally, religious and theological aspects as well. Then there is the literary shape of Wisdom, sometimes overplayed, we maintained. Many faces; *polypoikilos,* to be sure.

So to recognize Wisdom one must take account of all these characteristics and dimensions. Literary form or moral stance will not suffice to decide on the sapiential character of a person or composition. Sage and Deuteronomist can look very much alike; the Yahwist has been found akin to the sages for his "enlightened way of looking at man's environment, his interest in psychological factors, his distance from the world of the cult, etc."[5] But when one looks at all those etceteras, one finds a mentality that is vitally different—hence the need to look at all Wisdom's faces to be sure one is glimpsing a true sage.

A Unique Perspective

Then one can be confident of recognizing true Wisdom and not be deceived by mere form. Wisdom has a distinctive perspective,[6] a way of looking on the world, a *Weltanschaung* of its own, a distinctive sapiential view of reality—all reality. This is something comprehensive; at any rate, no other body of biblical literature has a wider view of reality. One therefore has reservations about accepting Sheppard's reduction of Wisdom (he writes "wisdom," but he is not thinking of the quality of being wise) to a hermeneutical construct, a theological category/concept/interpretation, a way of interpreting earlier Scripture.[7] Sirach and Baruch, the sole objects of Sheppard's study, do view Scripture differently from Jonah or Daniel, for instance, but also from Proverbs and Ecclesiastes. Wisdom, however, views everything distinctively; to stop short at one item in its line of vision is to sell it short.[8] Wisdom's perspective, even in the Bible, is more comprehensive than a scriptural hermeneutic.

That comprehensive perspective, with its many faces, enables us to distinguish Wisdom material from other bodies. It also discourages the application of simplistic definitions such as Whybray's nominal one on the basis of a mere word search.[9] Whatever may be true of individual similarities (such as we saw being made between Yahwist and sages above), a Wisdom perspective is clearly distinguishable from an apocalyptic perspective, a prophetic perspective, a historical perspective, the perspective of the Torah. Adoption of one form or another by bodies of literature (we saw in the previous chapter) does not alter their overall perspective. Even individual accents are not sufficient: a moralistic attitude does not bring Deuteronomists and sages together.[10] "Old wisdom" may differ from "late wisdom" in theological emphasis, as McKane insists;[11] yet if it is really atheological, as he would like to have accepted, it is no longer Wisdom, for there is no doubt of the theological face of Wisdom, implicit though it may be. Even a title like The Wisdom of Solomon does not remove misgivings about that work's less sapiential, more apocalyptic way of dealing with the real world; the perspective is flawed, no matter how much the author may want to claim the patronage of Solomon—-who "spoke of animals, and birds, and reptiles, and fish," we are assured in 1 Kings 4:33, unlike his namesake.

A Modern Sage

It seems to me we can take as our model in approaching Wisdom of the biblical period O. S. Rankin, who wrote in 1936 when, he laments, "appreciation of the Wisdom-writings cannot be said to be general."[12] He admitted people could be put off Wisdom for its canonical status and its "mundane and pedestrian" character. But he pressed on, arriving at a fine appreciation of Wisdom's perspective as distinct from other composition:

> In addition to the literary features which have led to the writings called Wisdom literature being grouped under that name as a class by themselves, there are certain characteristics which justify the use of the expression Wisdom-school of teachers. Though in-

terest in morality and religion is common to prophetic, apocalyptic, and other forms of composition, there is in the Wisdom writings a quite distinctive quality of mind, method, and outlook in respect of ethics and religious belief. Here we see growing stronger and more apparent as time advances a searching for first principles, the appreciation of these principles, a wrestling with the problems of faith, a criticism applied to the subjects of character and conduct, an observation of human nature, the atmosphere of discussion, the reliance upon reason along with the recognition of reason's limits. Here was prepared that deeper approach to the subject of ethics and religion which we observe in the Sermon on the Mount.[13]

Even with the positive encouragement that Rankin lacked, few of us have arrived at such an all-around appreciation of that "quite distinctive quality of mind, method, and outlook" that is the Wisdom perspective. Almost all of Wisdom's many faces are acknowledged above; today, with our sensitivity to the environment, we would probably also look for specific mention of the cosmic dimension. Rankin asks that within Israel's Wisdom literature there be included as well *The Letter of Aristeas, 4 Maccabees, Pirqe Aboth, Pseudo-Phocylides.*[14] Perhaps it takes a sage to appreciate one—someone with a like universalism, who before his time could also slip the limitations of canon and parochialism.

At least in terms of the Jewish and Christian Scriptures, Wisdom brought a wonderful and much-needed breadth of vision. May we see the growth of many sages among us today, and may we profit from their wisdom to help us glimpse Wisdom's many faces.

Notes

1. See my "Job in Search of Wisdom."
2. *Wisdom in the Old Testament Traditions*, 16.
3. P. Coelho; translated from the Portuguese (1988; San Francisco: HarperSanFrancisco, 1993) 133.
4. *Wisdom in Israel*, 294.

5. Von Rad, ibid., 294, n. 9.

6. See my "Perspective of Wisdom."

7. *Wisdom as a Hermeneutical Construct, passim.*

8. Childs, who enthuses over Sheppard's contribution, does well to add his own expansive codicil: "It also comes as no surprise that wisdom provides a fresh means of relating the human spirit with the divine" (*Biblical Theology of the Old and New Testaments*, 190). Sheppard had not ventured so far.

9. Cf. his *Intellectual Tradition in the Old Testament*, and comment on p. 5 above.

10. Zimmerli's caution in this regard is thus more dependable than Von Rad's readiness to stress similarities.

11. *Prophets and Wise Men, passim.*

12. *Israel's Wisdom Literature* (New York: Shocken, 1969) vii.

13. Ibid., ix.

14. Ibid., 1.

General Index

Index of Texts Cited

Index of Modern Authors